OUR
ULTIMATE
REFUGE

OUR ULTIMATE REFUGE

Formerly Titled *Baffled to Fight Better*

JOB AND THE **PROBLEM OF SUFFERING**

OSWALD CHAMBERS

AUTHOR OF **MY UTMOST FOR HIS HIGHEST**

DISCOVERY HOUSE PUBLISHERS®

Discovery House Publishers is affiliated with RBC Ministries,
Grand Rapids, Michigan.

Discovery House books are distributed to the trade exclusively by
Barbour Publishing, Inc., Uhrichsville, Ohio.

Requests for permission to quote from this book should be directed to:
Permissions Department, Discovery House Publishers,
P.O. Box 3566, Grand Rapids, MI 49501.

Scripture quotations are from the King James Version.

Library of Congress Cataloging-in-Publication Data

Chambers, Oswald, 1874-1917.
    [Baffled to fight better]
    Our ultimate refuge : Job and the problem of suffering /
Oswald Chambers.
        p. cm.
    Originally published: Grand Rapids, MI : Discovery House
    Publishers, [1997], c1990.
    ISBN 1-57293-198-1
1. Bible. O.T. Job--Criticism, interpretation, etc. 2. Bible. O.T.
Job--Devotional literature. 3. Suffering--Biblical teaching.
    4.Suffering--Religious aspects--Christianity. I. Title.
    BS1415.52.C53 2006
    223'.107--dc22

                                                    2006014377

Printed in the United States of America

08 09 10 11 12 / BP / 8 7 6 5 4 3 2

Contents

Publisher's *Foreword*   6

Foreword to the First Edition (1917)   8

Foreword to the Third Edition (1924)   10

Foreword from the Reprinted Edition (1947)   11

The Unseen Universe   13

Dazed and Amazed   18

The Passion of Pessimism   24

The Light That Failed   29

Out of the Depths   35

More Questions Than Answers   41

Agnosticism   49

Pretension   57

On the Trail   62

Much Ado About Nothing   69

The Frontiers of Despair   75

The Bitterest Hurt in Life   83

The Primal Clash   90

Parables   99

The Passion for Authority   108

The Passion for Reality   118

Locks vs. Keys   124

Disguise of the Actual   131

Notes   139

Publisher's Foreword

The well-known author of *My Utmost for His Highest* takes a very honest look at the book of Job and discovers the essence of the issue which has plagued mankind for centuries: "Why do the righteous suffer?" The problem of pain is an ancient one yet never more real than when faced by those of us living in the twenty-first century. All of the comforts of modern gadgetry have not dispelled the pain of our fallenness.

Chambers presents God as not only the *ultimate* refuge, but our *only* refuge. With characteristic insight he discusses our myths of self-sufficiency and eternal optimism, revealing their inadequacy when faced with the destruction of all that humankind values. Only with that sense of ultimate and utter loss do we come to admit that all we have is God.

The author does not approach his study of Job systematically. He does not dissect its theology or organize its doctrines. Rather, he analyzes its chronological development from Satan's challenge in the early chapters to the final climax of Job's restoration. He recognizes that in the fidelity of Job's despair there was hope because "Job was seeing God, for the first time in his life, as the only refuge. We know nothing about redemption or forgiveness until we crave for it." In the extremes of his life Job found that God was enough.

It is the publisher's hope that this new edition of *Our Ultimate Refuge* will bring hope and encouragement to you who are

in the midst of hurt and suffering. May you also, in your perplexities over the seeming injustices of life, learn to fight better.

—THE PUBLISHER

Foreword to the First Edition (1917)

This book is comprised of talks given nightly by Reverend Oswald Chambers to the men at the Imperial School of Instruction,[1] Zeitoun, Egypt, during the spring of 1917.

The one who spoke the words is now in the presence of the King, "serving Him day and night in His temple," and our prayer is that this book may serve to quicken in us all "a personal passionate devotion to Jesus Christ." Our Lord Himself was the one Lodestar in the life of my husband, and every recalling of him is an incentive to "follow his ways in Christ."

> *For himself*
> *So shadowed forth in every look and act*
> *Our Lord, without Whose name he seldom spoke,*
> *One could not live beside him and forget.*

B.C.[2]

EGYPT, 1917

Central Hall, Westminster, London, S.W.

It is with sincere pleasure that I write a few prefatory words to this last message from Reverend Oswald Chambers.

The Church of Christ has sustained a great loss in the Passing of our dear gifted Friend.

Reverend Oswald Chambers was a scholar, a burning Evangelist, a teacher of the Word of God, who taught in faith and verity.

He was full of the Holy Ghost, and turned many to the Lord. There is pathetic interest in these musings on the great drama of sorrow, which was also a true history.

Many will read them with tearful eyes as they recall their departed Author.

All, I am sure, will read with profit: may our Friend's lessons be messages of God to us all.

May we live in full consecration as he did, and whether we "fall asleep in Jesus," or remain till the Lord's return, may we be absolutely faithful!

—Dinsdale T. Young[3]

Foreword to the Third Edition (1924)

These talks were given in the Y.M.C.A. Huts, Zeitoun, Egypt,[4] to the men in the Egyptian Expeditionary Force during the early part of 1917. They were not given with the thought of publication, and the book is compiled from my own verbatim notes.

In November, 1917, God's call came to my husband for other service in His presence, and the idea came to me that to publish the talks he had been giving to the men in Egypt (and previously at the Bible Training College, London), would serve some purpose of God's, and the work was started with the prayer that the written messages might bring a knowledge of His truth to many as the spoken messages had ever done. This book was the first one to be published and was widely circulated amongst the men in Egypt and Palestine, many of whom had heard the talks given, an edition being also published in England at the same time.

I have a practically inexhaustible supply of notes, and other books will be published from time to time.

By his faith, he is speaking to us still. (Hebrews 11:4, Moffatt).

—B.C.

200 Woodstock Road, Oxford

October 1923

Foreword from the Reprinted Edition (1947)

These talks on Job by Oswald Chambers were given in the Y.M.C.A Hut Zeitoun Camp, Egypt in 1916. Night by night the men gathered, first to scan the chalked outlines on the blackboard, and then to take notes as the speaker gave a straightforward message within the scope of the headlines. So within about a month the whole book of Job was brought under review. It was with no thought of publication that Mrs. Chambers made a verbatim record of the lectures, but when the next year her husband passed from the earthly sphere, there was at hand material for the first edition of this book. In that and succeeding editions it has brought much light to many who have been faced with the tragic basis of our human life. Its message is as appropriate for this stage of the Second World War as it was for the First World War of this century. It sheds light on the abiding problems of pain, but above all it brings into view our Redeemer, and we too, like Job, may come to see the end purpose of the Lord that He is full of pity and merciful.

—David Lambert

The Unseen Universe

JOB 1:1–12

Man is not God but hath God's end to serve,
A master to obey, a course to take,
Somewhat to cast off, somewhat to become.
Grant this, then man must pass from old to new,
From vain to real, from mistake to fact,
From what once seemed good, to what now proves best.

—ROBERT BROWNING

The Record of the Natural (Job 1:1–5)

The Greatest Man in the East

His Goodness (v. 1)
His Grandeur (vv. 2–4)
His Graciousness (v. 5)

The Record of the Supernatural (Job 1:6–12)

The Scenery Behind the Seen

Sons of God (v. 6)
Satan and God (vv. 7–8)
Satanic Sneer About God (vv. 9–12)

It is in such a book as Job that many suffering souls will find consolation and sustaining, and this because no attempt is made to explain the *why* of suffering, but rather an expression is given to suffering which leaves one with the inspiration of an explanation in the final issue. The problem in connection with suffering arises from the fact that there is seemingly no explanation of it.

To say that Job was perfected by means of his sufferings is begging the question, for Job was perfect in moral and religious equipment before suffering touched his life. "Hast thou considered my servant Job, that there is none like him in the earth, a perfect and an upright man, one that . . . escheweth evil?" (Job 1:8). Job suffered "according to the will of God" (1 Peter 4:9); he never knew the preface to his story.

Verses 6–12 are a record of the supernatural; there is nothing familiar to our minds in them. The Bible deals with what no ordinary mind sees—the scenery behind the things that are seen. We have means of inferring the existence of a supernatural world only when it interferes with us. These verses refer to something that happened in the supernatural world, and it is what happened there that accounts for Job's sufferings; therefore the upset which came into the life of this great and good man is not to be laid to his account.

There is a difference between Satan and the devil which the Bible student should note. According to the Bible, man is responsible for the introduction of Satan: Satan is the result of a communication set up between man and the devil (see Genesis 3:1–5). When Jesus Christ came face to face with Satan He dealt with him as representing the attitude man takes up in organizing his life apart from any consideration of God. In the wilderness temptation the devil is seen in his undisguised character; only once did our Lord address the devil as "Satan"—"Then said Jesus unto him, Get thee hence, Satan. . . ." (Matthew 4:10). On another occasion Jesus said that self-pity was satanic—"But he turned, and said unto Peter, Get thee behind me, Satan. . . ." (Matthew 16:23).

The devil is the satanic adversary of God in the rule of man and Satan is his representative. Because a thing is satanic does not necessarily mean that it is abominable and immoral; our Lord said that "that which is highly esteemed among men is abomination in the sight of God" (Luke 16:15). Satan rules this world under the inspiration of the devil and men are peaceful, "when a strong man armed keepeth his palace, his goods are in peace" (Luke 11:21), there is no breaking out into sin and wrongdoing. One of the most cunning travesties is to represent Satan as the instigator of external sins. The satanically-managed man is often moral, upright, proud, and individual; he is absolutely self-governed and has no need of God.

Satan counterfeits the Holy Spirit. The Holy Spirit represents the working of God in a human life when it is at one with God through the redemption; in other words, "Holy Spirit" is the heredity brought into human nature at regeneration. When a man is born from above he has granted to him the disposition of Jesus, *Holy Spirit*, and if he obeys that disposition he will develop into the new manhood in Christ Jesus. If by deliberate refusal a man is not born again he is liable to find himself developing more and more into the satanic, which will ultimately head up into the devil.

"Then Satan answered the LORD, and said, Doth Job fear God for nought?" (Job 1:9). Verses 9–12 might be paraphrased in this way: Satan is represented as saying to God, "You are infatuated with the idea that man loves You for Your own sake; he never has and never will. Job, for instance, simply loves you because You bless and prosper him, but touch any one of his blessings and he will curse You to Your face and prove that no man on earth loves You for Your own sake."

It must be remembered what Job's creed was. Job believed that God prospered and blessed the upright man who trusted in

Him, and that the man who was not upright was not prospered. Then came calamity after calamity, everything Job believed about God was contradicted and his creed went to the winds. Satan's sneer is the counterpart of the devil's sneer in Genesis 3; there, the devil's object is to sneer about God to man; here, Satan's object is to sneer about man to God, he is "the accuser of our brethren"(Revelation 12:10).

Today there is in our midst a crop of juvenile skeptics, men who up to the time of the war[5] had had no tension in their lives, and as soon as turmoil embroiled them they flung over their faith and became cheap and easy skeptics. The man who knows that there are problems and difficulties in life is not so easily moved. Most of us get touchy with God and desert Him when He does not back up our creed (see John 6:60, 66). Many a man through this war has lost his form of belief in God and imagines that he has thereby lost God, whereas he is in the throes of a conflict which ought to give birth to a realization of God more fundamental than any statement of belief.

There are things in our heavenly Father's dealings with us which have no immediate explanation. There are inexplicable providences which test us to the limit, and prove that rationalism is a mere mental pose. The Bible and our common sense agree that the basis of human life is tragic, not rational, and the whole problem is focused for us in this book of Job. Job 13:15 is the utterance of a man who has lost his explicit hold on God, but not his implicit hold, "Though he slay me, yet will I trust in him." That is the last reach of the faith of a man. Job's creed is gone; all he believed about God has been disproved by his own experiences, and his friends when they come, say in effect, "You are a hypocrite, Job, we can prove it from your own creed." But Job sticks to it, "I am not a hypocrite, I do not know what accounts for all that has happened, but I will hold to it that God is just and that I shall yet see Him vindicated in it all."

God never once makes His way clear to Job. Job struggles with problem after problem, and providence brings more problems all the time, and in the end Job says, " . . . now mine eye seeth thee" (Job 42:5): all he had hung on to in the darkness was true, and that God was all he had believed Him to be, loving and just, and honorable. The explanation of the whole thing lies in the fact that God and Satan had made a battleground of Job's soul without Job's permission. Without any warning, Job's life is suddenly turned into desperate havoc and God keeps out of sight and never gives any sign whatever to Job that He *is*. The odds are desperately against God and it looks as if the sneer of Satan will prove to be true; but God wins in the end, Job comes out triumphant in his faith in God, and Satan is completely vanquished.

Will I trust the revelation given of God by Jesus Christ when everything in my personal experience flatly contradicts it?

Dazed and Amazed

Jesus, Whose lot with us was cast,
Who saw it out, from first to last: . . .
Would I could win and keep and feel
That heart of love, that spirit of steel.

I would not to Thy bosom fly
To slink off till the storms go by,
If you are like the man you were
You'd turn with scorn from such a prayer.

—WILFRID BRINTON

In the Whirlwind of Disaster

The Onslaught of Destruction (Job 1:13–19)

God gave Satan authority to interfere with all that Job possessed, "Behold, all that he hath is in thy power" (Job 1:12). All that a man possesses is at times not in the hand of God, but in the hand of the adversary, because God has never withdrawn that authority from Satan. The disasters that attend a man's possessions are satanic in their origin and not of the haphazard order they seem to be. When Jesus Christ talked about discipleship He indicated that a disciple must be detached from property and possessions, for if a man's life is in what he possesses, when disaster comes to his possessions, his life goes too (see Luke 12:15).

Satan had been allowed to attack Job's possessions; now his power is increased, and he is free to attack Job's personal inheritance directly. When a man is hit by undeserved destruction, the immediate result is a slander against God: "Why should God allow this thing to happen?"

There are people today who are going through an onslaught of destruction that paralyzes all our platitudes and preaching; the only thing that will bring relief is the consolations of Christ. It is a good thing to feel our own powerlessness in the face of destruction; it makes us know how much we depend upon God. In these days the outstanding marvel is the way mothers and wives have gone through sorrow, not callously, but with an extraordinary sense of hopefulness. One thing the war has done is to dispel all such shallow optimism as telling people to "look on the bright side of things"; or that "every cloud has a silver lining": there are some clouds that are black all through.

The Ordeal of Despair (Job 1:20–21)

Naked came I out of my mother's womb, and naked shall I return thither: the LORD gave, and the LORD hath taken away; blessed be the name of the LORD. (v. 21)

Facing facts as they are produces despair, not frenzy, but real downright despair, and God never blames a man for despair. The man who thinks must be pessimistic; thinking can never produce optimism. The wisest man that ever lived said that "he that increaseth knowledge increaseth sorrow" (Ecclesiastes 1:18). The basis of things is not reasonable, but wild and tragic, and to face things as they are brings a man to the ordeal of despair. Ibsen presents this ordeal. There is no defiance in his presentation; he knows that there is no such thing as forgiveness in nature, and that every sin has a nemesis following it. His summing up of life is that of quiet despair because he knows nothing of the revelation given of God by Jesus Christ.

"Blessed are they that mourn" (Matthew 5:4). Our Lord always speaks from that basis, never from the basis of the "gospel of temperament." When a man is in despair he knows that all his thinking will never get him out, he will only get out by the sheer creative effort of God, consequently he is in the right attitude to receive from God that which he cannot gain for himself.

The Ordination of Discretion (Job 1:22)

In all this Job sinned not, nor charged God foolishly.

The apostle James talks about "the patience of Job" (James 5:11), but "patience" is surely the last word we would have applied to Job! He confronts his friends with his scathing criticisms. Yet Job was never fundamentally impatient with God; he could not understand what God was doing, but he did not charge God with foolishness; he hung on to the certainty that God would yet be cleared, and so would he. Our Lord said that He was "meek and lowly in heart" (Matthew 11:29), yet meekness is not the striking feature He portrayed when He drove out those that sold and bought in the temple, and overthrew the tables of the money-changers. Our Lord was meek towards His Father's dispensations for Him, but not necessarily meek towards men when His Father's honor was at stake.

In the Wickedness of Desolation

The Sieve of Satan (Job 2:1–6)

In chapter 2 the veil is lifted from behind what is seen and the tragedy is explained. Job's possessions have gone, but he still holds to his integrity; now Satan conducts his sneer one bit nearer. The first sneer was to God—"Man only loves You because You bless him"; now Satan obtains permission to interfere with Job's intimate possessions, his sense of integrity and his health— "Behold, he is in thine hand; but save his life" (Job 2:6). The last stake of Satan is in a man's flesh.

There are times when a man's intimate personal possessions are under Satan's domination. The apostle Paul calls Satan "an angel of light" (2 Corinthians 11:14), he comes to a man whose personal possessions are being attacked and says—"You have lost the sense of the presence of God, therefore you must have back-slidden." There is a wicked inspiration in it; the thing underneath is the wickedness of desolation. Desolation is never a right thing; wrong things happen *actually* because things are wrong really. One of the dangers of fanaticism is to accept disaster as God's appointment, as part of His design. It is not God's design, but His permissive will. There is a vital moral difference between God's order and His permissive will. God's order is: no sin, no Satan, no sickness, no limitations. The unaided intellect of man recognizes this and says, "I will cut out sin and redemption and Jesus Christ, and conduct my life on rational lines."

Then comes the permissive will of God: sin, Satan, diffi-culty, wrong, and evil. And when desolation and disaster strike a man there is a wicked sting at the heart of it, and if he does not allow for the real thing behind it all he is a fool. We have to grasp God's order through His permissive will. A Christian must not lurk in the bosom of Christ because his thinking gives him a headache. It is moral and spiritual cowardice to refuse to face the thing and to give in and succumb. The greatest fear a Christian has is not a personal fear, but the fear that his hero won't get through, that God will not be able to clear His character. God's purpose is to bring "many *sons* unto glory" (Hebrews 2:10). Right through all the turmoil that is produced, and in spite of all Satan can do, this book of Job proves that a man can get through to God every time.

The Scourge of Suffering (Job 2:7–10)

The first outer court of a man's life is his flesh, and Job was smitten "with sore boils from the sole of his foot unto his crown" (v. 7). Then the wife of his bosom counselled him to "curse God, and die. But he said unto her, Thou speakest as one of the foolish women speaketh. What? shall we receive good at the hand of God, and shall we not receive evil? In all this did not Job sin with his lips" (vv. 9-10). That is where the scourge of suffering lies. When I suffer and feel I am to blame for it, I can explain it to myself; when I suffer and know I am not to blame, it is a harder matter; but when I suffer and realize that my most intimate relations think I am to blame, that is the limit of suffering. That is where the scourge of suffering lashed Job, the power of the sneer of Satan has come now into his most intimate relationships.

The Solitariness of Sorrow (Job 2:11–13)

Now when Job's three friends heard of all this evil that was come upon him, they came every one from his own place; . . . And when they lifted up their eyes afar off, and knew him not, they lifted up their voice, and wept; . . . So they sat down with him upon the ground seven days and seven nights, and none spake a word unto him: for they saw that his grief was very great.

Job's friends were hit desperately by the calamities that had overtaken Job because their creed was the same as his had been; and now if Job was a good man, as their own hearts told them he was, where was their creed? They were dumbfounded with agony, and Job was left without a consoling friend. The friends came slowly to the conclusion that their view of God was right, therefore Job must be wrong. They had the ban of finality[6] about their views, which is always the result of theology being put before God. The friends suffered as well as Job, and the suffering which comes from having outgrown one's theological suit is of an acute order. Job's attitude is, "I cannot understand why God has allowed these things to happen; what He is doing hurts desperately, but I believe that He is honorable, a God of integrity, and I will stick to it that in the end it will be made absolutely clear that He is a God of love and justice and truth."

Nothing is *taught* in the book of Job, but there is a deep, measured sense of someone understanding. This man was buffeted and stripped of all he held dear, but in the whirlwind of disaster he remained unblameable, that is, undeserving of censure by God.

The Passion of Pessimism

JOB 3

The world sits at the feet of Christ
Unknowing, blind, and unconsoled;
It yet shall touch His garment's fold,
And feel the heavenly Alchemist
Transform its very dust to gold.

—WHITTIER

Optimism is either a matter of accepted revelation or of temperament; to think unimpeded and remain optimistic is not possible. Let a man face facts as they really are, and pessimism is the only possible conclusion. If there is no tragedy at the back of human life, no gap between God and man, then the redemption of Jesus Christ is "much ado about nothing." Job is seeing things exactly as they are. A healthy-minded man bases his life on actual conditions, but let him be hit by bereavement, and when he has got beyond the noisy bit and the blasphemous bit, he will find, as Job found, that despair is the basis of human life unless a man accepts a revelation from God and enters into the kingdom of Jesus Christ.

The Irreparable Birth (Job 3:1–7)

After this opened Job his mouth, and cursed his day. . . . Let the day perish wherein I was born. (vv. 1, 3)

It is a sad thing that Job is facing, and it seems that the only reasonable thing he can do is to mourn the day of his birth. With some people suffering is imaginary, but with Job it has actually happened, and his curse is the real deep conviction of his spirit— "Would to God I had never been born!" The sense of the irreparable is one of the greatest agonies in human life. Adam and Eve entered into the sense of the irreparable when the gates of Paradise clanged behind them. Cain cried out, "My punishment is greater than I can bear" (Genesis 4:13). Esau "found no place of repentance, though he sought it diligently with tears" (Hebrews 12:17). There are things in life which are irreparable; there is no road back to yesterday.

Job's sense of the irreparable brought him face to face with the thing God was face to face with, and when a man gets there he begins to see the meaning of the redemption. The basis of things is not rational, common sense tells him it is not; the basis of things is tragic, and the Bible reveals that the only way out is through the redemption. In Job's case it was not a question of his being oversatiated with the pleasures of life, he was suddenly hit without any explanation; his days of prosperity and conscious integrity came to an abrupt end, and, worst of all, his belief in God was assailed.

Real suffering comes when a man's statement of his belief in God is divorced from his personal relationship to God. The statement of belief is secondary, it is never the fundamental thing. It is always well to note the things in life that your explanations do not cover. Job is facing a thing too difficult for him to solve or master; he realizes that there is no way out.

The Irresponsible Blunder (Job 3:8–13)

If you read a book about life by a philosopher and then go out and face the facts of life, you will find the facts do not come within the simple lines laid down in the book. The philosopher's line works like a searchlight does, lighting up what it does and nothing more, daylight reveals a hundred and one facts which the searchlight had not taken into account. There is nothing simple under heaven saving a man's relationship to God on the ground of the redemption; that is why the apostle Paul says, "I fear, lest by any means, . . . your minds should be corrupted from the simplicity that is in Christ" (2 Corinthians 11:3).

Reason is our guide among the facts of life, but it does not give us the explanation of them. Sin, suffering, and the Book of God all bring a man to the realization that there is something wrong at the basis of life, and it cannot be put right by his reason. Our Lord always dealt with the "basement" of life, i.e., with the real problem; if we only deal with "the upper story" we do not realize the need of the redemption; but once we are hit on the elemental line, as this war has hit men, everything becomes different. There are many men today who for the first time in their lives find themselves in the midst of the elemental with no civilized protection, and they go through appalling agony.

The war has put an end to a great deal of belief in our beliefs. Coleridge's criticism of many so-called Christians was that they did not believe in God, but only believed their beliefs about Him. A man up against things as they are feels that he has lost God, while in reality he has come face to face with Him. It is not platitudes that tell here, but great books, like the book of Job, which work away down on the implicit line. There are many things in life that look like irresponsible blunders, but the Bible reveals that God has taken the responsibility for these things, and that Jesus Christ has bridged the gap which sin made between God and man; the proof that He has done so is the cross. God accepts the responsibility for sin, and on the basis of the redemption men find their personal way out and an explanation.

The Invincible Blackness (Job 3:13–22)

These verses are not an indication of pain and suffering, but simply of blackness and a desire for quietness.

Wherefore is light given to him that is in misery, and life unto the bitter in soul; Which long for death, but it cometh not; and dig for it more than for hid treasures; Which rejoice exceedingly, and are glad, when they can find the grave? (vv. 20–22)

In the invincible blackness caused by Job's condition, death seems the only way out. In every age which has seen a great upheaval, the initial stage has always been marked by the advocacy of suicide, which is an indication of the agony produced by facing things as they are. The basis of things is wild. The only way you can live your life pleasantly is by being either a pagan or a saint. Only by refusing to think about things as they are can we remain indifferent.

The Inherited Baffling (Job 3:23–26)

The sense of being baffled is common, and Job is feeling completely baffled by God's dealings with him.

Why is light given to a man whose way is hid, and whom God hath hedged in?. . . I was not in safety, neither had I rest, neither was I quiet; yet trouble came. (vv. 23, 26)

We may not experience the sense of being baffled by reason of any terrific sorrow, but if we really face the teachings of Jesus Christ in the Sermon on the Mount honestly and drastically, we shall know something of what Job was going through. The teachings of Jesus Christ must produce despair, because if He means what He says, where are we in regard to it? "Blessed are the pure in heart" (Matthew 5:8)—blessed is the man who has nothing in him for God to censure. Can I come up to that standard? Yet Jesus says only the pure in heart can stand before God. The New Testament never says that Jesus Christ came primarily to teach men: it says that He came to reveal that He has put the basis of human life on redemption, that is, He has made it possible for any and every man to be born into the kingdom where He lives (see John 3:3). Then when we are born again His teaching becomes a description of what God has undertaken to make a man if he will let His power work through him. So long as a man has his morality well within his own grasp he does not need Jesus Christ: "For I came not to call the righteous, but sinners," said Jesus (Matthew 9:13). When a man has been hard hit and realizes his own helplessness he finds that it is not a cowardly thing to turn to Jesus Christ, but the way out which God has made for him.

There is a passion of pessimism at the heart of human life and there is no ointment for it; you cannot say, "Cheer up, look on the bright side"; there is no bright side to look on. There is only one cure and that is God Himself, and God comes to a man in the form of Jesus Christ. Through Jesus Christ's redemption the way is opened back to yesterday, out of the blunders and blackness and baffling into a perfect simplicity of relationship to God. Jesus Christ undertakes to enable a man to withstand every one of the charges made by Satan. Satan's aim is to make a man believe that God is cruel and that things are all wrong; but when a man strikes deepest in agony and turns deliberately to the God manifested in Jesus Christ, he will find Him to be the answer to all his problems.

The Light That Failed

JOB 4–5

We live in deeds, not years; in thoughts, not breaths;
In feelings, not in figures on a dial.
We should count time by heart-throbs. He most lives
Who thinks most—feels the noblest—acts the best.
Life's but a means unto an end—that end,
Beginning, mean and end to all things—God.

—Philip James Bailey

It is not what a man *does* that is of final importance, but what he *is* in what he does. The atmosphere produced by a man, much more than his activities, has the lasting influence.

The Premise of Precedent (Job 4:1–6)

Eliphaz is the first of the friends to emerge from their dumbfounded silence, and he starts out with the premise that God will never act any differently from the way He has always acted, and that man must not expect He will. The opening verses are a stately introduction to his theme:

Behold, thou hast instructed many, and thou hast strengthened the weak hands. Thy words have upholden him that was falling, and thou hast strengthened the feeble knees. But now it is come upon thee, and thou faintest; it toucheth thee, and thou art troubled. (vv. 3–5)

The precedent from which Eliphaz argues is that although Job has instructed many and been an upholder of the weak, now that he himself is going through such terrific suffering he must be wrong somewhere. Eliphaz reasons on the grounds that Job is experiencing the same kind of trouble as those whom he had previously comforted. This is not true. Job is suffering because God and Satan have made a battleground of his soul, without giving him any warning or any explanation. It is an easy thing to argue from precedent because it makes everything simple, but it is a risky thing to do. Give God "elbow room"; let Him come into His universe as He pleases. If we confine God in His working to religious people or to certain ways, we place ourselves on an equality with God. Job's suffering is not according to precedent; the thing that has struck Job had struck none of those whom he had instructed and comforted. It is a good thing to be careful in our judgement of other men. A man may utter apparently blasphemous things against God and we say, "How appalling"; but if we look further we find that the man is in pain, he is maddened and hurt by something. The mood he is talking in is a passing one and out of his suffering will come a totally different relationship to things. Remember, that in the end God said that the friends had not spoken the truth about Him, while Job had.

We are in danger of doing the same thing as Eliphaz; we say that a man is not right with God unless he acts on the line of the precedent we have established. We must drop our measuring-rods for God and for our fellow men. All we can know about God is that His character is what Jesus Christ has manifested; and all we know about our fellow men presents an enigma which precludes the possibility of the final judgment being with us.

The Presentation of Preconception (Job 4:7–21)

Eliphaz goes on to reason on a preconception that God blesses the good man, but does not bless the bad man.

Remember, I pray thee, who ever perished, being innocent? or where were the righteous cut off? Even as I have seen, they that plow iniquity, and sow wickedness, reap the same. (vv. 7–8)

Eliphaz takes his argument from nature: "For whatsoever a man soweth, that shall he also reap" (Galatians 6:7)—that God does not punish the upright, and that the innocent do not perish. That simply is not true, and it is this preconception which distorted Eliphaz' point of view. Preconceptions exist in our own head; if we start out with the preconception that God will never allow the innocent to perish and then we see a righteous man perishing, we will have to say, "You cannot be a righteous man, because my preconception tells me that if you were, God would never allow you to suffer; therefore you are proved to be a bad man." When Jesus Christ came on the scene the preconception of the historic people of God was this—"We are the constitution of God, Judaism is God's ordination, therefore You cannot be," and they crucified Him. Our Lord said that His Church would be so completely taken up with its precedents and preconceptions that when He came it would be "as a thief in the night"; they would not see Him because they were taken up with another point of view.

There are people who can silence you with their logic while all the time you know, although you cannot prove it, that they are wrong. This is because the basis of things is not logical, but tragic. Logic and reasoning are only methods of dealing with things as they are; they give no explanation of things as they are.

The Preaching from Prejudice (Job 5:1–16)

Prejudice means a judgment passed without sufficiently weighing the evidence. We are all prejudiced, and we can only see along the line of our prejudices. The way a prejudice works is seen clearly in Eliphaz: he knows God, and he knows how He will work—God will never allow the righteous to suffer, consequently when he sees the disasters in Job's life he passes judgment right off on Job and says he is not righteous. There is a saying of Bacon's to the effect that if prosperity is the blessing of the Old Testament, adversity is the blessing of the New[7]; and the apostle Paul says that "all that will live godly in Christ Jesus shall suffer persecution" (2 Timothy 3:1–2).

In every life there is one place where God must have "elbow room." We must not pass judgment on others, nor must we make a principle of judging out of our own experience. It is impossible for a man to know the views of Almighty God. Preaching from prejudice is dangerous, it makes a man dogmatic and certain that he is right. The question for each of us to ask ourselves is this: Would I recognize God if He came in a way I was not prepared for—if He came in the bustle of a marriage feast, or as a carpenter? That is how Jesus Christ appeared to the prejudices of the Pharisees, and they said He was mad. Today we are trying to work up a religious revival while God has visited the world in a moral revival, and the majority of us have not begun to recognize it. The characteristics that are manifested when God is at work are self-effacement, self-suppression, abandonment to something or someone other than myself, and surely there has never been more evidence of these characteristics than on the part of the men engaged in this war.

The Pedagogue of Priggishness[8] (Job 5:17–27)

Eliphaz is not only certain what God will do, but he asserts that what Job is going through is chastisement at the hand of God.

Behold, happy is the man whom God correcteth: therefore despise not thou the chastening of the Almighty: for he maketh sore, and bindeth up: he woundeth, and his hands make whole. (vv. 17–18)

But chastisement is a much lesser thing than the real problem of Job's life. The chief ingredient in chastening is that it is meant to develop us, and is a means of expression. The greatest element in the suffering of Job was not chastisement, but the supernatural preface to his story of which he knew nothing. If Eliphaz is right his evidence would prove that Job was a hypocrite; his attitude is that of a pedagogue of priggishness. Beware of priggishness as you would of poison. The danger of pseudo-evangelism is that it makes the preacher a "superior person," not that he is necessarily a prig,[9] but the attitude is produced by the way he has been taught.

When our Lord said to the disciples, "Follow me, and I will make you fishers of men" (Matthew 4:19), His reference was not to the skilled angler, but to those who use the drag-net—something which requires practically no skill; the point being that you do not have to watch your "fish," but you have to do the simple thing and God will do the rest. The pseudo-evangelical line is that you must be on the watch all the time and lose no opportunity of speaking to people, and this attitude is apt to produce the superior person. It may be a noble enough point of view, but it produces the wrong kind of character. It does not produce a disciple of Jesus, but too often it produces the kind of person who smells of gunpowder and people are afraid of meeting him. According to Jesus Christ, what we have to do is to watch the source and He will look after the outflow: "He that believeth on me, . . . out of his belly shall flow rivers of living water" (John 7:38).

Who are the people who have really benefited from you? They are never the ones who think they do, but those who are like the stars or the lilies, no notion of the prig about them. It was this form of pseudo-evangelism, so unlike the New Testament evangelism, that made Huxley[10] say—"I object to Christians: they know too much about God." Eliphaz can tell Job everything about God, but when we come to the facts of the case we find that the man who is criticizing Job is not fit to sit down beside him. Eliphaz was in a much better condition at the beginning when he did not open his mouth, then he was not a prig, but a man facing facts which had no explanation as yet.

If the study of the book of Job is making us reverent with what we don't understand, we are gaining insight. There is suffering before which you cannot say a word; you cannot preach "the gospel of temperament"; all you can do is to remain dumb and leave room for God to come in as He likes. The point for us is, "Do I believe in God apart from my reasoning about Him?" Theology is a great thing, so is a man's creed; but God is greater than either, and the next greatest thing is my relationship to Him.

Out of the Depths

Oh, the regret, the struggle and the failing!
Oh, the days desolate and useless years!
Vows in the night, so fierce and unavailing!
Stings of my shame and passion of my tears!

How have I knelt with arms of my aspiring
Lifted all night in irresponsive air,
Dazed and amazed with overmuch desiring,
Blank with the utter agony of prayer!

— F. W. H. MYERS[11]

A t this stage of his suffering Job portrays the terrific despair that can lay hold of a man; yet Job is not interested in himself, his is not the art of expressing the consciousness of every symptom of mind and heart characteristic of so many introspectionists today.

The Anatomy of Melancholy (Job 6:1–14)

Oh that my grief were throughly weighed, and my calamity laid in the balances together! (v. 2)

As previously stated, no sane man who thinks and who is not a Christian can be optimistic. Optimism, apart from a man's belief and his acceptance of Christianity, may be healthy-minded, but it is blinded; when he faces the facts of life as they are, uncolored by his temperament, despair is the only possible ending for him. There is a melancholy that is insane, it comes from having a fixed idea about things and is the result of a diseased brain; but Job's melancholy is the result of an intense facing of the things that have happened to him, and of his refusal to allow his religious beliefs to blind him to what he sees. Job refuses to tell a lie either for the honor of God or for his own comfort. When a man gets within the outskirts of the experience of Job's suffering and perplexity and is in touch with the problems at the heart of life, he will probably do one of two things—either tell a lie for the honor of God and say, "I must be much worse than I thought I was," or else accept a form of belief which does away with thinking. Most of us take our salvation much too cheaply. There is no hope for Job, and no hope for anyone on the face of the earth, unless God does something for him. One result of the war will be just this, that when a man faces things he knows, despair is inevitable unless there is room for God to perform His almighty acts. This line of things may sound foreign to us because we do not think, we are too contented with what we are; we have not been desperately hit. Job's melancholy is occasioned by his acceptance of the worst point of view, not a temperamental point of view.

The Anger Against Misunderstanding (Job 6:15–30)

My brethren have dealt deceitfully as a brook, and as the stream of brooks they pass away. (v. 15)

Job complains that his friends have "dealt deceitfully as a brook," i.e., they have answered his words and not his meaning (cf. Jeremiah 15:18—"wilt thou be altogether unto me as a liar, and as waters that fail?")

A Quaker friend of mine referring to a certain man said he did not like him because he did not hate properly. Job's anger seems to be of the order the apostle Paul mentions—"Be ye angry, and sin not" (Ephesians 4:26); his anger was against the misunderstanding of his friends, he had a right to expect that they would not misunderstand. The reason they misunderstood was that they took Job's words and deliberately denied the meaning which they knew must be behind them, and that is a misunderstanding not to be easily excused. It is possible to convey a wrong impression by repeating the exact words of someone else, to convey a lie by speaking the truth, and this is the kind of misunderstanding Job indicates his friends are guilty of. They have stuck steadfastly to his literal words and taken their standpoint not from God, but from the creed they have accepted; consequently they not only criticize Job and call him bad, but they totally misrepresent God. Job's complaint is not the shallow expression often heard—"No one understands me"; he is complaining of misunderstanding based on a misconstruction. He says in effect, "You have given me counsel when I did not ask for it; I am too greatly baffled and can only hold to what I am persuaded of, namely, that I have not done wrong; but I am indignant with you for not understanding."

In a crisis people quote the advice of Gamaliel—"For if this counsel or this work be of men, it will come to nought: but if it be of God, ye cannot overthrow it; lest haply ye be found even to fight against God" (Acts 5:38–39), that is, there is no use fighting against it; whereas the Christian standpoint should be one of positive anger when anyone is made to stumble. To remain indifferent when there is injustice abroad is to come under the curse of Meroz, who "came not to the help of the Lord . . . against the mighty" (Judges 5:23). A conscientious objector is not necessarily a

Christian. Conscience is a constituent in a natural man, but a Christian is judged by his personal relationship to God, not by his conscience.

The Anguish of Misery (Job 7:1–11)

My days are swifter than a weaver's shuttle, and are spent without hope. Therefore I will not refrain my mouth; I will speak in the anguish of my spirit; I will complain in the bitterness of my soul. (vv. 6, 11)

Misery is an exquisite degree of torture from which there seems no relief; it is very rare. Job suffered in this way, and many people are doing so today on account of the war. We all experience these things in a passing mood, but with Job it is no mood, he is facing the real basis of life. That is why the book of Job is included in the Bible. His words are not the expression of ordinary misery and melancholy, they are the expression of a man face to face with the foundation of human life, which is tragic. Every time Job opens his mouth he proves that the "bottom board" of rationalism is gone, there is nothing reasonable about what he is going through.

The war has proved that the basis of things is what Job discovered it to be—tragic, and men are being driven to realize the need for the redemption. Facing things as they are will reveal the justification of God in the redemption. No amount of sacrifice on the part of man can put the basis of human life right: God has undertaken the responsibility for this, and He does it on redemptive lines. Job's suffering comes from seeing the basis of things as they are; and, diseased and wild as Nietzsche was, his madness was probably from the same source. Imagine a man seeing hell without at the same time perceiving salvation through Jesus

Christ—his reason must totter. Pseudo-evangelism makes an enormous blunder when it insists on conviction of sin as the first step to Jesus Christ. When we have come to the place of seeing Jesus Christ, then He can trust us with the facing of sin.

In dealing with men like Job or the apostle Paul we must remember that we are dealing with men whom God uses to give us an estimate of things which we have never experienced. We cannot interpret Job in the light of our own moods; the problem of the whole world is mirrored for us in Job's experiences.

The Appeal For Mercy (Job 7:12–21)

Job gives utterance to a mood which is not foreign to us when he says, "Am I a sea, or a whale, that thou settest a watch over me?" (Job 7:12). In certain moods of anguish the human heart says to God, "I wish You would leave me alone, why should I be used for things which have no appeal to me?" In the Christian life we are not being used for our own designs at all, but for the fulfillment of the prayer of Jesus Christ. He has prayed that we might be one with Him as He is one with the Father, consequently God is concerned only about that one thing, and He never says "By your leave." Whether we like it or not, God will burn us in His fire until we are as pure as He is, and it is during the process that we cry, as Job did, "I wish You would leave me alone." God is the only being who can afford to be misunderstood; we cannot, Job could not, but God can. If we are misunderstood we "get about" the man as soon as we can. St. Augustine prayed, "O Lord, deliver me from this lust of always vindicating myself." God never vindicates Himself, He deliberately stands aside and lets all sorts of slanders heap on Him, yet He is not in any hurry.

We have the idea that prosperity, or happiness, or morality, is the end of a man's existence; according to the Bible it is something other, namely, "to glorify God and enjoy Him for ever.[12]" When a man is right with God, God puts His honor in that man's keeping. Job was one of those in whom God staked His honor, and it was during the process of His inexplicable ways that Job makes his appeal for mercy, and yet all through there comes out his implicit confidence in God. "And blessed is he, whosoever shall not be offended in me," said our Lord (Matthew 11:6).

More Questions Than Answers

JOB 8

If thou couldst empty all thyself of self,
Like to a shell dishabited,
Then might He find thee on the Ocean shelf,
And say—"This is not dead,"
And fill thee with Himself instead.
But thou art all replete with very thou,
And hast such shrewd activity,
That, when He comes, He says:—"This is enow
Unto itself—'Twere better let it be:
It is so small and full, there is no room for Me."

—T. E. BROWN[13]

Bildad differs from Eliphaz in his condemnation of Job: Eliphaz declares straight off that Job is wrong, while Bildad takes another line—that of asking questions; neither of them come anywhere near the reason for Job's suffering. There is an element of "Yes, but" in us all, and for most of us the problems that are nearly strangling a man have no meaning, they seem extravagant and wild. Bildad did not begin to detect where the real problem of Job's suffering lay, and we must beware in our attitude toward people who are suffering that we do not blunder by imagining our point of view to be the only one. Bildad puts Job off by asking questions. That is generally the way of the man who refuses to face problems.

The Complaint of "How" (Job 8:1–2)

Then answered Bildad the Shuhite, and said, How long wilt thou speak these things? and how long shall the words of thy mouth be like a strong wind?

Bildad turns attention away from what is making Job speak to his actual words—"Why do you talk so much?"—but he does not take the trouble to find out the reason. When we come across a foul-mouthed, blasphemous man any number of us are ready to reprove him but for the one who will try to discover why he speaks in that manner. Job is looking for someone who will understand what lies behind his talk, but he finds only those who are far removed from his problem.

To say that because Job lived in another time therefore what he went through does not apply to us, is an easy, artificial shifting of the ground. There are characteristics which are different, but the problems manifested in the book of Job remain the same to this day. According to consistent argument, the New Testament saint should be leagues ahead of the Old Testament saint, but in reality no character in the New Testament is superior to those in the Old Testament. The revelation of redemption given through our Lord Jesus Christ is retrospective in our day; in the Old Testament it is prospective. Job goes down to the heart of the problems that make the redemption necessary, while Bildad, with his incessant questioning and pious dealing with the problems, is really shirking the whole thing.

The Place of "Doth" (Job 8:3)

Doth God pervert judgment? or doth the Almighty pervert justice?

The trick of the sincere shirker is indicated in Bildad, which is always the result of being hit unexpectedly. We are all sincere shirkers, more or less; when we find ourselves suddenly discerned we turn the discernment off to something else for the time being (cf. John 4:16–20). In putting these abstractions before Job, Bildad is implying that Job's problem is not so difficult to understand: his suffering is caused by his own wrong-doing, and God's judgment is perfectly right. It is a trying thing to continue with a man who persists in giving an abstract supposition as a concrete fact.

The Philosophy of "If" (Job 8:4–6)

If thy children have sinned against him, . . . if thou wouldest seek unto God betimes, . . . if thou wert pure and upright. . .

The implication behind all these suppositions is: "Even if you are as wrong as Eliphaz has made out, you are not suffering so much as you imagine, and there is no big problem at the heart of things. God is not unjust, but you are, and that is the reason for it all." When problems are pressing very hard there is always someone who brings a suggestion of "if," or "but," or "how," to take us off the track. If our problems can be solved by other men, they are not problems but simply states of confusion. When we come to the real downright problems of life, which have no explicit answer except by the designer of life, we are exactly where Job was, and we can understand his petulance with those who tried to answer him. If Job's friends had remained dumb and reverent with what they did not understand, as they did during the first seven days, they would have been a great sustaining to him. They too would have approached the place Job ultimately reached and would not have been rebuked by God.

The "gospel of temperament" works very well if you are suffering only from psychological neuralgia, so to speak, and all you need is a cup of tea; but if you have a real deep complaint, the injunction to "cheer up" is an insult. What is the use of telling a woman who has lost her husband and sons in the war to "Cheer up and look on the bright side"? There *is* no bright side, it is absolute blackness, and if God cannot come to her help, truly she is in a pitiable condition. It is part of the role of a man to be honest enough to know when he is up against cases like this. A gospel based on preconceived notions is merely an irritant. Bildad had his creed and his notion of God: Job does not fit into these, therefore it is a bad outlook for Job—"My point of view of God cannot be wrong, therefore you must be."

The Pose of Platitude (Job 8:7–10)

For enquire, I pray thee, of the former age, and prepare thyself to the search of their fathers: . . . shall not they teach thee, and tell thee, and utter words out of their heart?

The line Bildad takes up in these verses is like a man telling the inmates of an asylum that it is better being sane than mad— but meantime they are mad! Bildad denies that Job is facing a problem never faced by his fathers. We are apt to forget that there is always an element in human suffering never there before. Tennyson puts this finely in "In Memoriam":

One writes that, "Other friends remain"
That "Loss is common to the race"—
And common is the commonplace,
And vacant chaff well meant for grain
That loss is common would not make

My own less bitter, rather more:
Too common! Never morning wore
To evening, but some heart did break.

There is a great deal in both joy and sorrow that is similar in everyone's case, but always one element entirely different; the one given to platitudes evades this. On the human side the only thing to do for a man who is up against these deeper problems is to remain kindly agnostic. The biggest benediction one man can find in another is not in his words, but that he implies: "I do not know the answer to your problem, all I can say is that God alone must know; let us go to Him." It would have been much more to the point if the friends had begun to intercede for Job; if they had said, "This is a matter for God, not for us; our creed cannot begin to touch it"; but all they did was to take to "chattermagging"[14] and telling Job that he was wrong. When God emerged, He put His imprint on what Job had said of Him, and His disapproval on what the friends had said.

If redemption is not the basis of human life, and prayer man's only resource, then we have "followed cunningly devised fables" (2 Peter 1:16). Over and over again during this war men have turned to prayer, not in the extreme of weakness, but of limitation; whenever a man gets beyond the limit he unconsciously turns to God. Eliphaz claimed to know exactly where Job was, and Bildad claims the same thing. Job was hurt, and these men tried to heal him with platitudes. The place for the comforter is not that of one who preaches, but of the comrade who says nothing, but prays to God about the matter.

The biggest thing you can do for those who are suffering is not to talk platitudes, not to ask questions, but to get into contact with God, and the "greater works" will be done by prayer (see John 14:12–13). Job's friends never once prayed for him; all they did was to try to prove a point to enrich their own creed out of his sufferings. We are not intended to understand life. Life makes us what we are, but life belongs to God. If I can understand a thing and can define it, I am its master. I cannot understand or define life; I cannot understand or define God; consequently I am master of neither. Logic and reason are always on the hunt for definition, and anything that cannot be defined is apt to be defied, rationalism usually defies God and defies life; it will not have anything that cannot be defined on a rational basis, forgetting that the things that make up elemental human life cannot be defined.

There are teachers today who play the fool on these elemental lines; they declare that they can give guidance, but they only succeed in doing a fathomless amount of harm. A man is a criminal for knowing some things, he has no right to know them. The primal curse of God was on Adam when he ate the fruit of the tree of the knowledge of good and evil. Adam was intended to know good and evil, but not by eating of the fruit of the tree; God wanted him to know good and evil in the way Jesus Christ knew it, namely, by simple obedience to His Father. None of us by nature knows good and evil in this way, and when we are born from above we have to take care that we deal with reverence with the elemental things underlying life.

The Point of "Can" (Job 8:11)

Can the rush grow up without mire? can the flag grow without water?

Bildad uses an argument from nature and he tries to make his argument consistent with his illustration. We are apt to run an illustration to death in logical sequence; the Bible never does. An illustration should simply be a window which does not call attention to itself. If you take an illustration from nature and apply it to a man's moral life or spiritual life, you will not be true to facts because the natural law does not work in the spiritual world. In the first place, a law is not a concrete thing, but a constructive mental abstraction whereby the human mind explains what it sees. God says, "And I will restore to you the years that the locust hath eaten" (Joel 2:25); that is not a natural law, and yet it is what happens in the spiritual world. In the natural world it is impossible to be made all over again, but in the spiritual world it is exactly what Jesus Christ makes possible. "Verily, verily, I say unto thee, Except a man be born again, he cannot see the kingdom of God" (John 3:3).

What is true is that as there *is* a law in the natural world so there *is* a law in the spiritual world, i.e., a way of explaining things, but the law is not the same in both worlds. Bildad takes his illustration from the rush and the flag and applies it to Job, but he is more concerned about being consistent with his illustration than with the facts of Job's experience. If you are a logician you may often gain your point in a debate and yet feel yourself in the wrong. You get the best of it in disputing with some people because their minds are not clever, but when you get away from your flush of triumph you feel you have missed the point altogether; you have won on debate, but not on fact. You cannot get at the basis of things by disputing. Our Lord Himself comes off second best every time in a logical argument, and yet you know that He has in reality come off "more than conquerors" (Romans 8:37). Jesus Christ lived in the moral domain and, in a sense, the intellect is of no use there. Intellect is not a guide, but an instrument.

The Practice of Piousness (Job 8:12–22)

*Behold, God will not cast away a perfect man, neither will
he help the evil doers. (v. 20)*

Bildad is cultivating the margin of his eyesight, so to speak.
This is a trick of the piousness not based on a personal relationship to God. Bildad is apparently speaking of an abstraction
while all the time he is criticizing Job—it is Job who is the hypocrite and the fraud. It is not meanness in Bildad that makes him
do this, but "limitedness"—he is "all replete with very thou."
Bildad has never seen God, while Job is getting near the place
where he will see Him. All the god Bildad has is his creed; if he
had known the real God he would have prayed to Him, and
would have recognized the facts that were too big for him. Whenever we put belief in a creed in place of belief in God, we become
this particular kind of nonsense. To "imply wrong by my right"
is the trick of every man who puts his creed before his relationship to God.

During this war many a man has come to find the difference
between his creed and God. At first a man imagines he has back-
slidden because he has lost belief in his beliefs, but later on he finds
he has gained God, i.e., he has come across reality. If reality is not
to be found in God, then God is not found anywhere. If God is
only a creed or a statement of religious belief, then He is not real;
but if God is, as the book of Job brings to light, one with whom a
man gets into personal contact in other ways than by his intellect,
then any man who touches the reality of things, touches God.

Agnosticism

JOB 9–10

Pour forth and bravely do your part,
O knights of the unshielded heart!
Forth and forever forward!—out
From prudent turret and redoubt,
And in the mellay charge amain,
To fall but yet to rise again.

—R. L. Stevenson

Agnosticism is not always the deplorable thing it is imagined to be. An acknowledged intellectual agnosticism is a healthy thing; the difficulty arises when agnosticism is not acknowledged. To be an agnostic means I recognize that there is more than I know, and that if I am ever to know more, it must be by revelation.

The Cosmic Refraction of God (Job 9:1–12)

If you accept Jesus Christ's presentation of God and then look at the present order of the material universe you will find what is meant by the phrase, "the cosmic refraction of God." Whenever God presents Himself in the present order of things, He appears refracted, that is, distorted to our reason; we cannot understand Him. When a man comes face to face with nature, God seems to be almighty against all his conceptions. God allows things in the cosmic world which are a refraction, they do not

49

continue in the straight, simple line my mind tells me they ought to take. Job says, in effect, "If God chooses to be almighty against me, where am I?" "If he will contend with him, he cannot answer him one of a thousand" (Job 9:3). The eccentric old poet, George Herbert, has a poem in which this phrase recurs—

> *Be not Almightie, let me say*
> *Against, but for me.*

The reason for Job's agony and distress is not a temperamental one; he has been brought to the heart of things and finds tragedy there, and a gap. The only way out is by means of the redemption; in the meantime Job is stating the perplexity as it appears to a man who is really beginning to think. Every one of us in our day and generation whether we have ever thought deeply or not, has faced this problem: If God is love, why does He allow the hawk to kill the sparrow? As Tennyson puts it— ". . . Nature, red in tooth and claw." Why does He allow one animal to feed on another? Why are nations allowed to fight each other? These are not passing perplexities but real puzzles, and the only thing to do is either to deny the facts or to confess we are agnostic. Job is up against the problem that things do not look as they should if God is the kind of God his implicit belief constrains him to declare He ought to be. Job's friends deny the facts; they won't have it that there is any perplexity, and they say to Job, "The reason God appears refracted is because you yourself are refracted."

The cosmic force makes God appear indifferent and cruel and remote, and if you become a special pleader of any particular creed you have to shut your eyes to facts. The only revelation which gives a line of explanation is that there is something wrong at the basis of things, hence the refraction. The apostle Paul says that creation is all out of gear and twisted; it is waiting "for the manifestation of the sons of God" (Romans 8:19). In the meantime, the problem remains.

Look at the world through either a microscope or a telescope and you will be dwarfed into terror by the infinitely minute or the infinitely great; both are appalling. When you touch the cosmic force, apart from the blinkers of intellect, there is a wild problem in it. Nature is wild, not tame. No man is capable of solving the riddle of the universe because the universe is mad, and the only thing that will put it right is not man's reason, but the wisdom of God which is manifested in the redemption of Jesus Christ. A Christian is an avowed agnostic intellectually; his attitude is, "I have reached the limit of my knowledge, and I humbly accept the revelation of God given by Jesus Christ."

The Conscious Resurgence of Goodness (Job 9:13–20)

How much less shall I answer him, and choose out my words to reason with him? Whom though I were righteous, yet would I not answer, but I would make supplication to my judge. (vv. 14–15)

"Resurgence" is used here to mean the reconsideration of a former judgment. The majority of us start out with the belief that God is good and kind, and that He prospers those who trust in Him. Job believed this, but he has a conscious resurgence against that belief now, and it is Job's goodness, not his badness, which makes him reconsider things. There are things in the experience of us all which call for a revision of our credal findings about God; there are other elements that will not come into our declaration as to the kind of being He is.

Eliphaz and Bildad have no problem along this line; their one aim is to convict Job of being a scroudrel. The sign of dishonesty in a man's creed is that he finds out defects in everyone save himself—"It is not possible for me to be mistaken in my view of God." Bildad and Eliphaz would not admit that they could be wrong; they had the ban of finality about their views. Trouble always arises when men will not revise their views of God. Bildad tells Job that if he was upright he would not suffer as he did. Job maintains—"I am upright, and yet everything has gone wrong with me." Job stuck steadily to facts, not to consistency to his creed. Over and over again a man is said to be a disbeliever when he is simply outgrowing his creed. It is a most painful thing for a man to find that his stated views of God are not adequate. Never tell a lie for the honor of God; it is an easy thing to do. Job refuses a presentation of God which does not face the facts; he has no skepticism about God, no hesitation about His existence, but he does tirade all the time against the way in which He is being presented.

The Concentrated Reaction of Grief (Job 9:21–35)

For he is not a man, as I am, that I should answer him, and we should come together in judgment. Neither is there any daysman betwixt us, that might lay his hand upon us both. (vv. 32–33)

Job is giving expression to a new conception of God; his hope is that an umpire, a daysman, will arise who will not only justify God, but also justify him. "My creed does not do this," he says, "neither does my experience, or my way of looking at things." It was grief that brought Job to this place, and grief is the only thing that will; joy does not, neither does prosperity, but grief does. The great factor in the life of Jesus Christ, the redeemer of the world, is this very thing—". . . Yet it pleased the LORD to bruise him" (Isaiah 53:10). Once grief touches a man he is full of reaction, he says spiteful things because he is hurt, but in the end grief leads a man to the right point of view, namely, that the basis of things is tragic. As long as I am happy and things go well, I say what a famous philosopher said—"This is the best of all possible worlds." It plainly is not, and the Bible reveals why it is not. The world as God originally designed it, was the best of all possible worlds, but it has now become the worst of all possible worlds; in fact, the Bible reveals that it could not be any worse than it is. Individual men who take the wrong line get worse, but the world itself cannot get worse. Grief brings a man to see this more quickly than anything else, and he longs for an umpire who will hold the scales.

There is no use telling Job that there is no God or that he has not suffered: he has had too much experience of God and of suffering. It is useless to tell him that his creed is the umpire that arbitrates between himself and God: it leaves too much unsolved. Job is the type of man who could never rest in the church, or in the Scriptures; he needs living reality. The man who rests in a creed is apt to be a coward and refuse to come into a personal relationship with God. The whole point of vital Christianity is not the refusal to face things, but a matter of personal relationship, and it is the kind of thing that Job went through which brings a man to this issue.

The Conceptions for Rejection (Job 10:1–17)

Job's utterances are the last word in the expression of certain forms of grief. These particular verses are stately and terrific; Job is trying to state to his own mind why God seems to have rejected him, and also why he should reject the way God is being presented to him—

Thou knowest that I am not wicked; and there is none that can deliver out of thine hand. Thine hands have made me and fashioned me together round about; yet thou dost destroy me. (vv. 7–8)

All along Job bases his conceptions on the facts which he knows, and this is the only thing to do, although many of us would rather tell a lie for the honor of God than face the facts. A fanatic is one who entrenches himself in invincible ignorance. Job will not accept anything that contradicts the facts he knows; he is not melancholy, he does not say God is cruel, he simply states the facts—"It looks as though God is rejecting me without any reason, all the facts go to prove this and I am not going to avoid them." Job will not lay a flattering unction to his soul on the line of expediency. No man ever puts a stumbling-block in the way of others by telling the truth; to tell the truth is more honoring to God than to tell a lie. If God has done something for you, you will know it unmistakably, but if He has not, never say He has for the sake of other people. Job sticks to facts, that is what confuses his friends; but in the end Job is brought face to face with God.

The Case for Refuge (Job 10:18–22)

Are not my days few? cease then, and let me alone, that I may take comfort a little, before I go whence I shall not return, even to the land of darkness and the shadow of death. (vv. 20–21)

"I see no way out," says Job. He lies down, not in weakness, but in absolute exhaustion. Job is not sulking, but saying that unless God will be a refuge for him, there is no way out, death is the only thing. In every crisis of life, as represented in the Old Testament as well as in the teaching of our Lord, this aspect of God is emphasized—"God is our refuge" (Psalm 46:1). Yet until we are hit by sorrow, it is the last thing we seek for God to be. There is a difference between the weakness of refusing to think and the weakness that comes from facing facts as they really are. Job is seeing for the first time that God is the only refuge, the only way out for him; yet he cannot get at Him through his creed, it is all confusion; the only thing to do is to fling himself on God.

It is this aspect of God which is at the basis of the redemption. When a man gets convicted of sin (which is the most direct way of knowing that there is a problem at the basis of life), he knows that he cannot carry the burden of it; he also knows that God dare not forgive him; if He did, it would mean that man's sense of justice is bigger than God's. If I am forgiven without being altered, forgiveness is not only damaging to me, but a sign of unmitigated weakness in God. Unless it is possible for God's forgiveness to establish an order of holiness and rectitude, forgiveness is an ordinary and abominable thing.

The human problem is too big for a man to solve, but if he will fling himself unperplexed on God he will find Him to be the kind of refuge Job is referring to. We know nothing about the redemption or about forgiveness until we are enmeshed by a personal problem; then we begin to understand why we need to turn to God, and when we do turn to Him He becomes a refuge and a shelter and a complete rest. Up to the present Job has had no refuge anywhere; now he craves it. When a man receives the

Holy Spirit, his problems are not altered, but he has a refuge from which he can deal with them; before, he was out in the world being battered, now the center of his life is at rest and he can begin, bit by bit, to get things uncovered and rightly related.

Pretension

JOB 11

I have not knowledge, wisdom, insight, thought.
Or understanding, fit to justify
Thee in thy work, O Perfect. Thou hast brought
Me up to this—and, lo! what thou hast wrought,
I cannot call it good. But I can cry—
"O enemy, the maker hath not done:
One day thou shalt behold, and from the sight wilt run."
—GEORGE MACDONALD

Stirring of Self-Respecting Indignation
(Job 11:1–4)

Then answered Zophar the Naamathite and said, Should
not the multitude of words be answered? and should a man
full of talk be justified? (vv. 1–2)

Zophar is manifesting the linguistic characteristic of Job. He begins by accusing Job of using a "multitude of words" (Job 11:2) thus blinding his mind to the point at stake. If you are annoyed with someone, notice how uncomfortably conscious you are that there is an element in him you cannot reach, and rather than allow the recognition of that element you work yourself up into self-respecting indignation. Zophar has come to the conclusion that Job is wrong, his creed is wrong, and "I alone am justified." This trick of stirring up self-respecting indignation is a very common subterfuge when we are embarrassed by a problem involving our self-respect. The temptation comes to yield to the pretentious mood, and we use terms of righteous indignation to condemn the thing we are not guilty of, while all the time we may be guilty of tenfold worse.

Superficial Invocation (Job 11:5–10)

But oh that God would speak, and open his lips against thee; and that he would shew thee the secrets of wisdom. . . . Canst thou by searching find out God? canst thou find out the Almighty unto perfection? (vv. 5–7)

Another trick of pretentious religion is to appeal to God in order to back up a position which is obviously questionable. Here, Zophar calls God in as his ally in his attack on Job. We do it in our way of praying; our invocations and iterations often spring from false emotions; they are not spontaneous. Most of us mouth diction before God; we do not pray; we say in prayer what we ought to say, not what is actually natural to us to say. It may sound very interesting and noble, but it is not our own, it is mere sounding brass and clanging cymbals, there is no reality in it.

Another form of superficial invocation affects the idea that God is punishing our nation for certain wrongs, instead of feeling the presence of something more profound. When we are facing problems we must see to it that we are reverent and silent, for the most part, with what we do not understand. The invocation of God is an exercise of the finest spiritual mood, and we are rarely in a sufficiently exalted state of mind for it. To invoke on the assumption that we know God, comes near to blasphemy.

Self-Consciousness of Serious Instruction
(Job 11:11–15)

If iniquity be in thine hand, put it far away, and let not wickedness dwell in thy tabernacles. For then shalt thou lift up thy face without spot; yea, thou shalt be steadfast, and shalt not fear. (vv. 14–15)

Zophar tries to instruct Job on an entirely false basis; he declares that Job will never get wisdom. "For vain man would be wise, though man be born like a wild ass's colt" (Job 11:12). This is all the length Zophar gets in dealing with a man who towers leagues above him! First, he stirs up self-respecting indignation, then he takes a religious turn, then an instructive turn, which puts the wrong self on top at once. The characteristic of this kind of instruction is that it is self-conscious. The most valuable instruction in moral life never comes from people who consciously instruct us, for we are not taught morally as we are intellectually. Confusion always results if we take the method of instruction used in intellectual life and apply it to moral life, and make certain people moral instructors. It is an abortion for any human being to dare to put himself in the position of a moral superior to another man, and this is what Zophar did with Job.

No man is consciously a moral superior to another man; if he is superior intellectually that is largely a matter of upbringing. The real basis of moral instruction lies much deeper down, namely, in God, and God instructs us along the line symbolized by the Christian sacrament, which means the real presence of God being conveyed to us through the common elements. God uses children, and books, and flowers in the spiritual instruction of a man, but He seldom uses the self-conscious snob who consciously instructs. The "Zophar" type has recurred all through the Christian centuries—the man who assumes he knows, and frequently the average man is led to say, "If experts in spiritual matters do not know these things, who am I that I should?" There are no experts in spiritual matters as there are in scientific matters. The spiritual expert is not that way consciously because the very nature of spiritual instruction is that it is unconscious of itself; it is the life of a child, manifesting obedience, not ostentation. Our Lord describes the spiritual expert in Matthew 18:4— "Whosoever therefore shall humble himself as this little child, the same is greatest in the kingdom of heaven."

Self-Complacency of Sentimental Integrity
(Job 11:16–20)

Because thou shalt forget thy misery, and remember it as waters that pass away: and thine age shall be clearer than the noonday; thou shalt shine forth, thou shalt be as the morning. (vv. 16–17)

Zophar is the type of a demagogue, the man who rules with his tongue. Any kind of absolute creed ends where Zophar ended—on the sentimental line, where things reach a pitch of enthusiastic presentation not based on facts. The sentimental line blinds man's thinking by an ecstasy of thought; it enables an orator to awaken human sentiment and sympathy, but in dealing with trouble it proves a false line; it gives impertinent advice to a man who is broken-hearted. Zophar implies that he knows exactly the kind of integrity that will stand before God and before man.

Self-respecting indignation nowadays is not on the "Zophar" line, but on the anti-Zophar, i.e., the anti-religious. Before the war it was not religious but irreligious nonsense that was prevalent. Men pretended they were not religious while secretly they were.

If you are a religious person of the "Zophar" type and can work up sufficient religious indignation, you will come to the conclusion that you and God must go together, it is quite impossible for you to be mistaken; then you will begin to instruct others on the same line, and will inevitably end by placing things in a totally false light.

On the Trail

JOB 12–14

True religion is betting one's life there is a God.

—Donald Hankey

The Charge of Intolerance (Job 12:1–5)

And Job answered and said, No doubt but ye are the people, and wisdom shall die with you. But I have understanding as well as you; I am not inferior to you; yea, who knoweth not such things as these? (vv. 1–3)

Job is speaking in a mood of annoyance, he rebels against the intolerance of his friends who do not give him credit for having any common sense. If we talk with a man who is dealing with the fundamentals, he may appear to pay no attention to any common-sense explanation we offer because his deep is beyond our deep, so we instantly credit him with having no common sense and get back to our own shallows. The friends charge Job with a lack of seeing the obvious, and Job replies, "I am facing things you have not begun to dream about; why don't you either plunge into the deeps with me, or else keep silent, if you cannot tell me what to do?" A religious view which causes a man to deal only with the shallow side has the ban of finality about it.

Common Sense of Irrefutable Inference (Job 12:6–25)

Who knoweth not in all these that the hand of the LORD

hath wrought this? In whose hand is the soul of every living thing, and the breath of all mankind. (vv. 9–10)

Job accuses the friends of telling lies for the honor of God. That is the danger of putting theology first; it leads a man to tell a lie in order to be consistent with his point of view. Job is speaking not with the view of disproving God, but of proving that the religious conceptions of these men are not right. The things Job states are commonsense, obvious things, and they flatly contradict the creed he had believed, and which his friends are pushing down his throat. Are we going to remain true to our religious convictions or to the God who lives behind them?—true to our denominational view of God or to the God who gave the denomination its initial inspiration? Are we going to be mere sticklers for the theological statement? In the ecclesiastical history of Scotland many a man has gone to martyrdom rather than let his theology go. The organized Church is up against these things today.

Theology is tested by history and logic; religion must be tested by experience.

Job's creed has crumbled into ruins, "therefore," he says, "I leave my creed, but I deny that I have left God." In a theological dispute the theologian is apt to put his point of view in the place of God. "But if any man seem to be contentious, we have no such custom" (1 Corinthians 11:16) says the apostle Paul. Only one man in a thousand can maintain his spiritual life and controvert; he may increase his intellectual vim, but he does not increase his spiritual grasp of things. Dr. Alexander Whyte[15] put this better than any other when he said:

> Oh, the unmitigated curse of controversy! Oh, the detestable passions that corrections and contradictions kindle up to fury in the proud heart of man! Eschew

controversy, my brethren, as you would eschew the entrance to hell itself. Let them have it their way; let them talk; let them write; let them correct you; let them traduce you; let them judge and condemn you; let them slay you. Rather let the truth of God suffer itself, than that love suffer. You have not enough of the divine nature in you to be a controversialist. "He was oppressed and He was afflicted (Isaiah 53:7) yet He opened not His mouth; He is brought as a lamb to the slaughter, and as a sheep before its shearers is dumb, so He openeth not His mouth." "Who when He was reviled, reviled not again (1 Peter 3:23-24) when He suffered, He threatened not; . . . by whose stripes ye were healed." "Heal me," prays Augustine, again and again, "of this lust of mine of always vindicating myself."

We start out with the notion that God is an almighty piece of ourselves, but God can never be on the side of any individual; the question to ask is—"Am I on God's side?" In 2 Thessalonians 2, Paul talks about the invincible ignorance of fanaticism and he says that if a man is deluded, he is to blame. On the other hand Job says, "I am not going to say that my former definition of God is true; God must be true, but I find that the way I have expounded Him is not true." This put Job on the right track to find God. Are we on the trail of God, or on the obstinate, intolerant line, where we argue for our statements instead of for the truth? Does our religion put us on the line of understanding the revelation of God, or is it merely a blind authority? It is a good thing to take stock of the things which common-sense inferences and religion cannot explain.

The Conception of Invincible Ignorance (Job 13:1–12)

What ye know, the same do I know also. (v. 2)

This verse is a description of the fanaticism which builds on one point of view only and is determinedly ignorant of everything else. This is the thing Job rages against all the time—"God must be other than you have stated because of what I have experienced," and Job is right. It is possible to build logical edifices on a theological position and at the same time to prove in practical life that the position is wrong. For example, on the metaphysical line the predestinations of God seem clear, but our conception of those predestinations may prove dangerously false when we come to the actual facts of life.

The theological view ought to be constantly examined. If we put it in the place of God we become invincibly ignorant, that is, we won't accept any other point of view, and the invincible ignorance of fanaticism leads to delusions for which we alone are to blame. The fundamental things are not the things which can be proved logically in practical life.

Watch where you are inclined to be invincibly ignorant, and you will find your point of view causes you to break down in the most vital thing. An accepted view of God has caused many a man to fail at the critical moment, it has kept him from being the kind of man he ought to be, and only when he abandons his view of God for God Himself, does he become the right kind of man.

The Consecration of Instinctive Integrity (Job 13:13–28)

Hold your peace, let me alone, that I may speak, and let come on me what will. Wherefore do I take my flesh in my teeth, and put my life in mine hand! Though he slay me, yet will I trust in him. (vv. 13–15)

Job feels that in spite of all that is happening, God's integrity remains, and his own integrity. He cannot explain his sufferings by saying, "I am being punished because I have done wrong," or, "I am suffering because I needed to be perfected." The friends have accused Job of being a hypocrite and imply that he is also an atheist, but just at this very time Job gives expression to the most sublime utterance of faith in the whole of the Old Testament— "Though he slay me, yet will I trust in him." "Though He, whom you are misrepresenting, and whom I cannot state in words— though He slay me, I will trust in the fact that He is full of the integrity I believe Him to be, and I will wait for Him. I will face my own common-sense integrity, and dedicate my instinctive sense of God's integrity, and in the end I know that both will work out into one."

Always remain true to facts and to the intuitive certainty that God must be just, and do not try to justify Him too quickly. The juggling trick tries to justify God for allowing sin and war. Sin and war are absolutely unjustifiable, and yet the instinct of every Christian is—"I know that in the end God will justify Himself." Meantime you can only justify Him by a venture of faith which cannot be logically demonstrated.

The Consciousness of Implicit Infirmity (Job 14)

O that thou wouldest hide me in the grave, that thou wouldest keep me secret, until thy wrath be past, that thou wouldest appoint me a set time, and remember me! If a man die, shall he live again? all the days of my appointed time will I wait, till my change come. (vv. 13–14)

Job has discovered that the basis of things is tragic, not logical. "I know I am weak and there are facts in my life and in human history which I cannot explain, but because of my conscious infirmity I know that God will see me through it all and out the other side; meanwhile I refuse to accept a creed which misrepresents God, and also misrepresents me." To get there means a man is on the right trail.

Job's integrity remains as well as his conscious infirmity, and also the sense that he is not entirely to blame for his sinfulness. No man is held responsible by God for having an heredity of sin: what God holds a man responsible for is refusing to let Jesus Christ deliver him from it when he sees that that is what He came to do (see John 3:19).

Judged by average theology, many of Job's utterances sound far from right, yet in reality they are full of reverence. He is saying that in any statement about God there must be some indication that will justify Him in allowing human beings to be weak—"Your statement of God is not only untrue to man, but blasphemously untrue to God." Job states the facts of human experience, and that there seems to be an unsatisfactory end to life—"Just when I was going to grasp the thing and find the fulfillment of all my desires, I am cut off." There are countless men like that today; just when life was at its best and highest, suddenly they are swept clean off.

We get an expression of Job's meaning in verses 13–22 when we say of a man—"Well, he is dead now, and although he did not come up to the standard of our orthodox religion, we will leave him in the hands of a merciful God!" That is a subterfuge. Job states the facts and he is strong on the point that he will get to the place where he will see God justified in what He has allowed to happen. Never take a suspended judgment as final, but watch for the chance of getting fresh light on the matter. It is never sufficient to take a mental safety valve as the end of the matter. Many problems which arise from a man's instinctive integrity have not been answered; no theological statement can make answer to them, and we have to watch that we do not accept any statement which our instinctive nature tells us is a lie. We have our guide in Jesus Christ; we must never accept a view of God which contradicts what He manifested—"I am the way, the truth and the life" (John 14:6). The vital thing is to get on the trail of a personal relationship to God, and then use the facts of experience and of revelation to bring us to a consideration of things which satisfies our nature, and until it is satisfied, don't say it is. "I will stick to it that God is a God of love and justice, and I look forward to the time when I shall see it manifestly." We have no business to say piously, "Oh, I leave it with God." God will have us discern what He is doing, but it takes time because we are so slow to obey, and only as we obey do we perceive morally and spiritually.

Much Ado About Nothing

JOB 15

A pill to cure an earthquake. . . .

—G. K. Chesterton

There is nothing more ludicrous than the way in which some folk try to soothe sorrow and deal with trouble in other lives. Eliphaz makes out that Job's problems are not what he thinks they are; he tries to wear down Job's opposition by saying a lot of nothing with terrific emphasis. One can almost hear him choking with indignation: "What knowest thou, that we know not? . . ." (Job 15:9). Then follows the revealing of the unconscious egotism of the orthodox credist, dictatorially asserting the character of God (vv. 14–16). Then, like a theological buzzard, he sits on the perch of massive tradition and preens his ruffled feathers and croaks his eloquent platitudes. There is no trace of the fraud in Eliphaz, he vigorously believes his beliefs, but he is at a total loss to know God. Eliphaz represents the kind of nonsense that results from remaining true to conviction instead of to facts which dispute the conviction. The difference between an obstinate man and a strong-minded man lies just here: an obstinate man refuses to use his intelligence when a matter is in dispute, while a strong-minded man makes his decision after having deliberately looked at it from all standpoints, and when opposed, he is willing to give reasons for his decision.

The Weapons of the Temporizing Mind (Job 15:1–6)

Then answered Eliphaz the Temanite and said, Should a wise man utter vain knowledge, and fill his belly with the east wind? Should he reason with unprofitable talk? or with speeches wherewith he can do no good? (vv. 1–3)

A temporizing mind is one that takes its position from immediate circumstances and never alters that position. Eliphaz says that Job is simply pretentious; he sees in Job what he is himself. The weapon of a temporising mind is sarcasm. There is a difference between sarcasm and irony (cf. Job 12:1–3). Sarcasm is the weapon of the weak man; the word literally means to tear flesh from the bone. Both Isaiah and the apostle Paul make free use of irony, but they never use sarcasm. If a weak man is presented with facts he cannot understand, he invariably turns to sarcasm.

Eliphaz addresses a "man of straw," but all the time he purports to be talking to Job. First, he takes the scolding turn—"All you say about the suffering you are going through is much ado about nothing." Scolding is characteristic of the mind which is in a corner and does not see the way out; it falls back therefore to its own entrenched position. No one damns like a theologian, nor is any quarrel so bitter as a religious quarrel. If God can be summed up in a phrase—and Eliphaz and every man with a creed holds that He can be—then there is the ban of finality about the view: "What I say is God"; and this is the essential nature of religious tyranny. Up to the time of the war, God, to many a man, was merely his own theological statement of Him; but now his religious forms of belief have been swept away and for a while he says—"I have lost my faith in God." What has happened is that though he has lost his faith in his statement of God, he is on the way to finding God Himself. Never be afraid if your circumstances dispute what you have been taught about God; be willing to examine what you have been taught, and never take the conception of a theologian as infallible; it is simply an attempt to state things.

The Weight of the Traditional Manner (Job 15:7–13)

Art thou the first man that was born? or wast thou made before the hills? Hast thou heard the secret of God? and dost thou restrain wisdom to thyself? What knowest thou, that we know not? what understandest thou, which is not in us? (vv. 7–9)

When once the sledgehammer of tradition is brought to bear there is nothing more to say—"With us are both the gray-headed and the very aged men, much elder than thy father" (Job 15:10). Eliphaz says to Job—"Do you imagine that you have a setting of the problem which has never been dealt with before?" The Pharisees adopted this method with Jesus. Our Lord claimed that the law and the prophets were until Himself. "Ye have heard that it was said by them of old time, . . . but I say unto you. . ." (Matthew 5:21-22, 27-28). The Pharisees said, "We have all the weight of history behind us and the lore of tradition, consequently the constitution of God is with us and not with You; You are devil-possessed and a sinner," and they put Him to death. That is the traditional manner at its worst.

The "Eliphaz" method has hindered more souls in developing the life with God than almost any other thing, because very few men are willing to say: "Yes, I have a restatement of the problem which has never been dealt with traditionally." When once the weight of what was known in the past is brought to bear, it crushes the life out of what is going on in the present. If the traditional manner has any weight at all, it should make men courteous with the problems which are recent. Paul's advice to Timothy was—"Let no man despise thy youth" (1 Timothy 4:12). "Don't try to make up for your youth by dogmatism and talk, but see that you walk in such a manner that you are an example to the believers." No really wise, liberal-minded person ever needs to say, "Remember how old I am."

Traditional belief has the root of the matter in it, but its form is often archaic. We begin our religious life by believing our beliefs, we accept what we are taught without questioning; then when we come up against things we begin to be critical and we find that however right those beliefs are, they are not right for us because we have not bought them by suffering. Job's experiences and his suffering made him restate his beliefs. It is absurd to tell a man he must believe this and that; in the meantime he cannot. The traditional manner sits on the safety valve of every new type of experience. After the war, the redemption will need to be restated theologically. Redemption must be seen to be God's "bit," not man's. A man cannot redeem himself. At present "redemption" is not in the vocabulary of the average earnest Christian man. When the traditional believer hears men talk as they are doing, he is apt to get scared and to squash the life out of what, behind its insufficient expression, is going to be a re-illumination of traditional truth. If Eliphaz had been wise he would have seen what Job was getting at—"Job is facing something I do not see; I don't understand his problem, but I will treat him with respect." Instead of that he said, "According to my traditional belief, you are a hypocrite, Job."

The Ways of the Theological Method (Job 15:14–16)

Behold, he putteth no trust in his saints; yea, the heavens are
not clean in his sight. How much more abominable and filthy
is man, which drinketh iniquity like water? (vv. 15–16)

Theology is the science of religion, an intellectual attempt to
systematize the consciousness of God. If we take the doctrine of
the Trinity (which is a noble attempt of the mind of man to put
into a theological formula the Godhead as revealed in the Bible)
and say—"That is God," every other attempt at a statement of
the Godhead is met by a sledgehammer blow of finality. My theology has taken the place of God and I have to say—"That is
blasphemy." Theology is second, not first; in its place it is a hand-
maid of religion, but it becomes a tyrant if put in the first place.
The great doctrines of predestination and election are secondary
matters, they are attempts at definition, but if we take sides with
the theological method we will damn men who differ from us
without a minute's hesitation. Is there any form of belief which
has taken the place of God with me? We only believe along the
line of what we conceive of God, and when things happen con-
trary to that line, we deny the experience and remain true to our
theological method. Job is on the right trail.

The Words of the Tragedy-Monger (Job 15:17–35)

I will shew thee, hear me; and that which I have seen I will
declare. (v. 17)

Eliphaz empties all the vials of his wrath on Job, he takes the
facts of Job's life and colors them, then states them again as "a

man of straw." He pictures the terrific tragedy which is likely to happen to his "man of straw," and drives it home with—"Thou art the man" (2 Samuel 12:7). If Job is right, Eliphaz must be wrong, so he has to come to the conclusion that Job is a hypocrite, the worst of bad men, because what his creed declares to be the portion of a bad man, has come to Job. This accounts for the tirade of Eliphaz.

As a product of shallow evangelical teaching, people are led to fool themselves into believing that they are what they know perfectly well they are not; whereas the New Testament says if a man has the Holy Spirit it will show itself in fruit—"Wherefore by their fruits ye shall know them" (Matthew 7:20). There are any number of men who suddenly realize the shallowness of persuading themselves that they are what they are not, and they long for reality.

The standard for God cannot be experience; the standard is what Jesus Christ has revealed about God. If anything we may be told about God contradicts the manifestation given by Jesus Christ, we are at liberty to say, "No, I cannot believe that." Things have been taught about God which are seen to be diabolical when viewed in the light of our Lord's revelation of Him. Remain steadfastly true to what you have learned, and when you have to suspend your judgment, say it is suspended. This was Job's attitude all through. "Your creed distorts the character of God, but I know in the end He will prove to be all that I trust Him to be, a God of love and justice, and absolutely honorable."

The Frontiers of Despair

Then as I weary me and long and languish,
  Nowise availing from that pain to part
Desperate tides of the whole great world's anguish
Forced thro' the channels of a single heart,
Straight to thy presence get me and reveal it,
  Nothing ashamed of tears upon thy feet,
Show the sore wound and beg thine hand to heal it,
  Pour thee the bitter, pray thee for the sweet.

—F. W. H. Myers

Up till now we have seen Job as a sane pessimist, but now we find him on the frontiers of despair. A man may get to the point of despair in a hundred and one different ways, but when he does get there, there is no horizon. In everything else there is hope that a dawn may come, but in despair there is no hope of anything brighter, it is the most hopeless frontier a human mind can enter without becoming insane. An insane person is never despairing, he is either immensely melancholy or immensely exalted. Despair is the hopelessness that overtakes a sane mind when it is pushed to the extreme in grief.

The Revolt Against Pose (Job 16:1–5)

Then Job answered and said, I have heard many such things: miserable comforters are ye all. (vv. 1–2)

Job ironically takes on the pose which Eliphaz adopted, the pose of the superior person. Eliphaz has scolded Job and said that he is suffering because he is a bad man and a hypocrite. Job recognizes that Eliphaz does not begin to understand his problem, and he revolts against pose. It is difficult to evade pose in religious life because it is of the nature of unconscious priggishness. If you have the idea that your duty is to catch other people, it puts you on a superior platform at once and your whole attitude takes on the guise of a snob. This too often is the pose of the earnest religious person of today. Of all the different kind of men one meets the preacher takes the longest to get at, for this very reason; you can get at a doctor or any professional man much more quickly than you can a professionally religious man.

The religious pose is based, not on a personal relationship to God, but on adherence to a creed. Immediately we mistake God for a creed, or Jesus Christ for a form of belief, we begin to patronize what we do not understand. When anyone is in pain the thing that hurts more than anything else is pose, and that is what Job is fighting against here. No one revolts against a thing without a reason for doing so, not necessarily a wrong reason, because revolt is of a moral order. If we come across a counterfeit, reality is sure to be found somewhere. Job is up against the religious pose of men who do not begin to understand where his sorrow lies.

The Recapitulation of Pain (Job 16:6–22)

Job's honesty and his freedom from cowardice come out very clearly; he would not say he was guilty of what he knew he was not guilty. He says, "I am not suffering because I have committed sin; I do not know why I am suffering, but I know that is not the reason." The majority of us would have caved in and said, "Oh, well, I suppose I am worse than I thought I was." What looks like revolt against God may really be not against God at all, but against the presentation being given of Him.

The Psychology of It (Job 16:6–8)

Though I speak, my grief is not asswaged: and though I forbear, what am I eased? But now he hath made me weary: thou hast made desolate all my company. (vv. 6–7)

Many forms of grief find relief in expression—"the garment of words expressing the thing," but Job says that he cannot get any relief from his grief through expressing it. Not one of his friends can endure him; they believe he is desolate because God has left him. Every line of Job's experience seems psychologically to justify their judgment of him, and yet Job knows that what they say is not the explanation.

The Providence of It (Job 16:9–15)

God hath delivered me to the ungodly, and turned me over into the hands of the wicked. I was at ease, but he hath broken me asunder. (vv. 11–12)

These verses describe in mideastern terms the providence of Job's pain; everything has come out against him. "God seems to have engineered everything dead against me; the inner circumstances and the outer are all the same—God has beset me behind and before like a wild beast; everything in my providential setting and my human life goes to prove that my pain is the outcome of my sin."

The Pathos of It (Job 16:16–22)

O earth, cover thou not my blood, and let my cry have no place. My friends scorn me: but mine eye poureth out tears unto God. O that one might plead for a man with God, as a man pleadeth for his neighbour! When a few years are come, I shall go the way whence I shall not return. (vv. 18, 20–22)

This is not the pathos of a whining beggar who "puts it on" in order to awaken sympathy. Job's recounting of his suffering is not the expression of self-conscious pathos; he is stating for his own sake that he is sane, that he is in despair, and, so far as he can see, he is perfectly justified in being pessimistic.

There are many things like this as the outcome of this war, and we have to be careful lest we take on the religious pose, or the evangelical pose, or the denominational pose, or any pose that is not real, when we come across suffering in which there is no deliverance and no illumination. The only thing to do is to be reverent with what we do not understand. The basis of things is tragic; therefore God must find the way out, or there is no way out. Human reasoning and a human diagnosis of things will do exactly what Job's friends did, namely: belittle the grief.

The Recognition of Predestiny (Job 17)

If we look for understanding from a person and do not get it, the first feeling is one of revolt and indignation against him; but when we begin to examine things, we may find that after all he is not to blame for his density. It is this element that increases the suffering of Job, while at the same time it clears him from condemnation. Everything at the back of his life and of his creed, goes to justify the conclusion he has come to.

In the Density of Men (Job 17:1–4)

For thou hast hid their heart from understanding. (v. 4)

When we look for our friends to understand, and find they do not, we accuse them of being dense. In grief the sufferer frequently declares that no one on earth can assist him. This is sometimes a pose, but Job is seeing that his friends' density does not lie with them, but with the fact of predestination. There are some kinds of suffering and temptation and sorrow no one can sympathize with, and by means of them a man gets on to the solitary way of life. It is not the suffering of a man who has done wrong and knows it; it is an isolation in which no one can sympathize, God alone can come near.

The suffering of Job is accounted for by the fact that God and Satan had made a battleground of his life, and he is beginning to discover that it is God who has closed up the understanding of his friends. Satan has declared that Job does not love God for Himself, but only for His blessings, and now everything in the way of shelter and comradeship and sympathy has been completely stripped from Job, and he sees that God must have allowed it. This is the deepest line Job has come to as yet, but he still clings to it that God is honorable. "I have lost my family, my wealth, my friends, the consolation of my creed—I have lost everything to which a man can at all look for comfort; yet, though he slay me, I will trust in him" (Job 13:15). This is supreme despair, along with extraordinary confidence in God who meantime looks like a moloch.[16]

In the Discretion of Men (Job 17:5–10)

Upright men shall be astonied at this, and the innocent shall stir up himself against the hypocrite. But as for you all, do

*ye return, and come now; for I cannot find one wise man
among you. (vv. 8, 10)*

Job is recounting the fact that his experiences of sorrow and
difficulty have so come about that the wise element of discretion in
men must make them pass judgment against him. Everything
seems against him: not only his creed, but the ordinary wisdom of
men. There is nothing more agonizing to a man who knows his
own integrity than to find that the best people leave him alone, not
because they do not know why he suffers, but because they are sure
he is more in the wrong than he says, and their view is backed by
their own discretion and knowledge. As in the case of the density
of men, this discretion must not be laid at the door of men, but at
the predestiny of the way human wisdom is fixed. The predestiny
of human wisdom is rationalism. Any number of things happen
which are not reasonable, and human discretion is apt to say that
the man who suffers unreasonably is to blame; and when it is
pointed out that the basis of things is without reason, men say that
is only a passing difference. The Bible reveals that the basis of
things is not reasonable, but tragic. When a man is driven to the
bottom, he gets to the tragedy, not to the reason; he is alone with
God, and if God does not see him through, despair is the only
place for him. The more deeply and earnestly and directly a man
thinks, the more he finds what Solomon says is true—"he that
increaseth knowledge increaseth sorrow" (Ecclesiastes 1:18). It is
not Job's disposition that brings him to a pessimist's point of view,
but his plain sanity; he refuses to say that his pessimism is a mood;
optimism *is* a mood. If God does not see Job through, Satan has
won his wager; if God does not come on the scene somewhere, it is
a forlorn hope, and Satan will have proved that no one loves God
for His own sake. Everything a man can rely upon has disappeared,
and yet Job does not curse God; he admits that his former creed is

not right, neither are his friends right, yet he declares steadily that in the end God will be justified.

In the Despair Before Men (Job 17:11–16)

Job cannot hide his despair. For unfathomable pathos, verse 11 is unequalled in any language under heaven:

My days are past, my purposes are broken off, even the thoughts of my heart.

A certain type of religious hypocrisy makes men hide what they feel, but Job has come to the place where he cannot hide it—"I cannot pretend that I am comforted of God," he says. If only Job could have taken on the pose that he had the comfort of God, his friends would not have challenged him, but he says, "I have no comfort; I do not see God, neither can I talk to Him; all I know is that my creed and former belief must be wrong. I do not know what to accept, but I am certain God will prove that He is just and true and right, and I refuse to tell a lie in order to help Him out."

This attitude of religious faith is finely expressed by the Psalmist—"Then will I go unto the altar of God, unto God my exceeding joy" (Psalm 43:4). This is sublime faith, the faith that Jesus demanded of John the Baptist. ". . . And blessed is he, whosoever shall not be offended in me" (Matthew 11:6). Will I stick to it, without any pretence or nonsense, that God is righteous, although everything in my actual experience seems to prove that He is cruel? Most of us are hypocrites, we are too afraid to state the thing as Job did. We say right out, "God is cruel to allow me to go through this, and I refuse to believe in Him any more." Job stuck to his point that when everything was known it would not be to God's dishonor, but to His honor.

Because of this war, a great number of men in lesser degree have arrived at the place Job has got to, their creeds about God have gone, and it would be the height of absurdity to pretend that their former beliefs of God are true as they see Him now. It does not follow because a man has lost belief in his beliefs that therefore he has lost faith in God. Many a man has been led to the frontiers of despair by being told he has backslidden, whereas what he has gone through has revealed that his belief in his beliefs is not God. Men have found God by going through hell, and it is the men who have been face to face with these things who can understand what Job went through. All the impatience and irritation against the religious life, so called, is accounted for on the same line as Job's revolt against religious pose—"If they would only stop their pose and face facts as they are; be reverent with what they don't understand, and assist me in my faith in God." Job's friends were in the right place when they sat with him dumbfounded for seven days; they were much nearer God then than afterwards. Immediately they took up the cudgels for God[17] they took on a religious pose, lost touch with the reality of actual experience, and ended in being pompous.

The Bitterest Hurt in Life

JOB 18–20

Nay but much rather let me late returning
  Bruised of my brethren, wounded from within.
Stoop with sad countenance and blushes burning.
  Bitter with weariness and sick with sin,—

. . . .

Safe to the hidden house of thine abiding
  Carry the weak knees and the heart that faints,
Shield from the scorn and cover from the chiding,
  Give the world joy, but patience to the saints.

—F. W. H. MYERS

The bitterest hurt in life is to be wounded in the house of your friends; to be wounded by an enemy is bad enough, but it does not take you unawares, you expect it in a measure. "My kinsfolk have failed, and my familiar friends have forgotten me. All my inward friends abhorred me: and they whom I loved are turned against me" (Job 19:14, 19).

The Removal of the Atmosphere of Comradeship (Job 18)

There is always an intangible something which makes a friend, it is not what he does, but what he is. You feel the better for being in the presence of some men. Job is suffering because his friends have turned against him; he has lost the atmosphere of comradeship. He has no explanation for what he is going through, no line of exonerating God.

The Dignity of Withdrawal (Job 18:1–4)

Then answered Bildad the Shuhite, and said, How long will it be ere ye make an end of words? mark, and afterwards we will speak. (vv. 1–2)

In this withdrawal of comradeship there is an acuteness of suffering which is difficult to state. Job is hurt, and his friends not only tackle his belief, but they have withdrawn all support from him. The sympathy which is reverent with what it cannot understand is worth its weight in gold. The friends have stopped giving this kind of sympathy to Job, instead they say, "We know why it is you suffer." By sticking to his creed a man is able to withdraw with dignity simply because there is so much he does not see.

Bildad is certain that Job is wrong and he is right, and the puzzling thing is that Bildad can prove his statements, while Job has to remain silent. This is one of the biggest stings in life. When a man gets to reality he has to get there alone, there is no comradeship. He may have had comradeship up to a certain point, then he is told, "Now we have to leave you, you are out of bounds." The men who act like this have the logic of it on their side, but the man who is face to face with facts knows that logic is only an attempt to explain facts, it does not give us the facts. The man who does not believe that the basis of things is tragic may get the best of it in argument, but the man who gets the best of it in fact is the one who believes in God yet has to remain inarticulate.

Bildad describes the worst man he can think of, and Job says, "All this has happened to me, and you say therefore I must be a bad man, but I say I am not. You have the logic of your creed, while I have the reality of my experience. The God of your creed is one who would make me an atheist. The God who will explain my experience I have not yet found, but I am confident there is such a God, and meantime I refuse to accept your counterfeit of Him."

There are countless experiences like Job's today; men are being called atheists who are not atheists at all but are simply rebelling against the presentation of God which is being thrust upon them. If to accept a presentation of God means the denial of things he knows to be facts, a man is in a better case who says with Job, "I will not accept an explanation of God which makes me call a fact not a fact."

The Discourse in the Withdrawal (Job 18:5–21)

Yea, the light of the wicked shall be put out, and the spark of his fire shall not shine. Surely such are the dwellings of the wicked, and this is the place of him that knoweth not God. (vv. 5, 21)

A man has to cover his retreat somehow, and Bildad withdraws in a cloud of rhetoric; his description of the wicked man is a covert description of Job in his present condition. He recounts what Job has gone through and makes it the experience of an accomplished hypocrite—"I have satisfied my mind that you are a hypocrite; you are suffering because you are bad." Bildad airs his complete knowledge of the psychology of wickedness as God must deal with it, but evidently with as complete an ignorance of God as of man. His indignation with Job is petty, you can almost hear him puffing with righteous annoyance. The friends' speeches prove that when providence or suffering contradicts any form of credal belief, the holder of the creed becomes vindictive in trying to justify what is threatened, and no longer discerns the truth.

The Reaction of the Affection of Courage (Job 19)

The Appeal of Discouragement (Job 19:1–5)

Then Job answered and said, How long will ye vex my soul, and break me in pieces with words? (vv. 1–2)

"Discouragement is disenchanted egotism" (Mazzini),[18] i.e., the heart knocked out of self-love. Job had been in love with his creed, now belief in his creed is gone and he is completely at his wits' end, and from the center of his discouragement he makes his appeal to the men whom he had a right to expect would stand by him. "You take the side of the providence of God," he says, "which undoubtedly seems my enemy." This chapter is not only an expression of real agony and sorrow, but also of the stout integrity which will not allow itself to tell a lie for the honor of God. "God seems to be my enemy providentially," says Job, "and you say it is because I am bad; but I say that that is not the reason."

The Account of Desolateness (Job 19:6–20)

Know now that God hath overthrown me, and hath compassed me with his net. Behold, I cry out of wrong, but I am not heard: I cry aloud, but there is no judgment. (vv. 6–7)

Job's statements are not colored, he simply states what has happened to him—everything has gone and no explanation has been given him. There is no bright side to some troubles. There is no reasonable hope for countless lives on account of this war, and it is shallow nonsense to tell them to "cheer up"; life to them is a hell of darkness of the most appalling order. The one who preaches at such a time is an impertinence, but the one who says "I don't know why you are going through this, it is black and desperate, but I will wait with you," is an unspeakable benediction and sustaining. Job has no one to do this for him, his one-time friends simply add to his bitterness; they too have been hit along the line of their creed, and they are indignant and talk only on the religious line.

The Agony of Dereliction (Job 19:21–29)

Have pity upon me, have pity upon me, O ye my friends; for the hand of God hath touched me. For I know that my redeemer liveth, and that he shall stand at the latter day upon the earth. (vv. 21, 25)

The question of immortality is not necessarily implied in Job's words; he is stating that he believes a time will come when an umpire will arise who will expound to him what he is going through—to the justification of God as well as of himself. It is heroism almost unequaled to say, as Job did, "Though he slay me (Job 13:15), I will stick to it that God is a God of love and justice and truth. I see no way out at all, but I will remain true to my belief that when the whole thing is known God will not be condemned." All through Job refuses to take the easy way out along the line of his former creed.

The Recession of the Apprehension of Communion (Job 20)

The withdrawal of your most intimate friend with the conviction that you are wrong, means the loss of the atmosphere of comradeship and all that is represented by the closer intimacies of communion.

The Disdain of the Offended (Job 20:1–3)

Then answered Zophar the Naamathite, and said, I have heard the check of my reproach, and the spirit of my understanding causeth me to answer. (vv. 1, 3)

Zophar speaks with dignity, but dignity is not an indication of discernment. Zophar has listened to Job's words but not to the spirit of them; he is ashamed of the attitude his former friend has taken. A retreat from comradeship is nearly always covered by a terrific amount of utterance either in writing or speech. Bildad withdraws with descriptions; Zophar gives a formal discourse as to why he turns on Job with disdain.

The Discourse of the Offensive (Job 20:4–29)

Knowest thou not this of old, since man was placed upon earth, that the triumphing of the wicked is short, and the joy of the hypocrite but for a moment? (vv. 4–5)

One point of mercy is that the friends do not put the curse on Job directly. Cursing with us is only profane language, an expression and no more, but in the case of the curse of an Arab or a Hebrew the curse lies in the words themselves: if the curse is uttered it is impossible, according to their conviction, but that it shall fall. Zophar is uttering this kind of curse, only indirectly, and it gives his words tremendous power. The power of the spoken word accounts for the prominent place given in the Bible to prophesying and preaching.

Job's strong utterances are not against God, but against the statements of his former creed. The man who will stand true to God behind the expression of his creed is true to his belief *in God*, instead of to the presentation of Him which is in dispute. If you listen to a man who has been sorely hit, he may utter what, to you who have not been hit, sounds blasphemous. Job's claim is that his friends ought to have known that it was not imagination that made him speak as he did, but the fact that he had been desperately hard hit. The only way out for Job is not on the line of reason, but on the line of implicit confidence, such as he expresses in chapter 13—"Though he slay me, yet will I trust in him" (Job 13:15).

The Primal Clash

JOB 21–25

If we are going to understand the ordinary run of human life we must take into account the extraordinary experiences and tragedies. One reason for the futility of pseudo-evangelism is that we have taken the mediocre man, the average man, as the one best able to expound Christian experience. Christianity does embrace the weakest and the feeblest, but it is the men of exceptional experiences, such as Job or the apostle Paul, who make clear the basis of things. The "Primal Clash" means that we are down to the foundation of things.

The Realizing Sense of Perverseness (Job 21)

What is the Almighty, that we should serve him? and what profit should we have, if we pray unto him? God layeth up his iniquity for his children: he rewardeth him, and he shall know it. Behold, I know your thoughts, and the devices which ye wrongfully imagine against me. How then comfort ye me in vain, seeing in your answers there remaineth falsehood? (vv. 15, 19, 27, 34)

It is soul certainty that the world needs, even more than sound principles—not soul facility, but soul certainty, not ready religion, but sure.

—Dr. Forsyth[19]

Job persists in stating that the basis of things is not clear or easy to understand. "It is absurd to say, as you are doing," he says, "that God punishes the evil man and looks after the good, there is so much perversity at the basis of things that that explanation won't do." The friends give this explanation because they are true to their creed, and Job says, "I held the same creed as you do until I came to my great trouble." Their creed was based on sound principles, but what is needed is a sound relationship at the basis of things. When things are suddenly altered by bereavement or by some tension in personal experience, we find ourselves wonderfully at home with what Job says. There is a wildness about things, and we revolt against the people who explain everything on the basis of sound principles. They have everything ready at hand, and can tell you just where everyone goes wrong; but Job's contention is that when a man is face to face with things as they are, easy explanations won't do, for things are not easy; there is a perverseness all through. If Job is not right in his contention, then the redemption is "much ado about nothing."

The Reasoning Severity of Pharisaism (Job 22)

Then Eliphaz the Temanite answered and said, Can a man be profitable unto God, as he that is wise may be profitable unto himself? Acquaint now thyself with him, and be at peace: thereby good shall come unto thee. (vv. 1–2, 21)

Many a gross Pharisee is a mighty moralist and he believes himself sincere with it. The deadliest Pharisaism is not hypocrisy, it is the unconscious Pharisaism of unreality.

—Dr. Forsyth

The nature of Pharisaism is that it must stand on tiptoe and be superior. The man who does not want to face the foundation of things becomes tremendously stern and keen on principles and on moral reforms. A man who is hyper-conscientious is nearly always one who has done something irregular or who is morbid; either he is close on the verge of lunacy, or he is covering up something wrong by tremendous moral earnestness along certain lines of reform. A Pharisee shuts you up, not by loud shouting, but by the unanswerable logic he presents; he is bound to principles, not to a relationship. There is a great amount of Pharisaism abroad today, and it is based on "devotee-ness" to principles. Devotion to a cause is the great mark of our day, and in religion it means being devoted to the application of religious principles. A disciple of Jesus Christ is devoted to a person, not to principles.

Job's experience flatly contradicts the creed of this particular Pharisee, Eliphaz, so he jumps on Job. His words are eloquent and his charges terrific; he sums up all the facts and informs Job that he has maltreated the innocent, wronged the widow, and starved the orphan—

> Is not thy wickedness great? and thine iniquities infinite?
> For thou hast taken a pledge from thy brother for nought,
> and stripped the naked of their clothing. Thou hast not
> given water to the weary to drink, and thou hast withholden
> bread from the hungry. (vv. 5–7)

This is always the dodge of a Pharisee, whether he is a demagogue or a religious man, he must make a moral issue somewhere. If he can rouse up a passion for a neglected principle, it is exactly what he wants, but there is no reality in it. The Pharisaism of our Lord's day was based on the principles of Judaism, and when

Jesus Christ came the Pharisees did not recognize Him but said, "You are a hypocrite, we can prove it." Many of the religious phases of today do not touch reality, but only the Pharisaic insistence on a certain form of sound doctrine, and the man who is up against things finds nothing but chaff. Every denominationalist is certain that the crowd who does not agree with what "we" call our sound principles must be wrong; he never imagines that the "Job" type of man can be right with God. When God spoke to Eliphaz, as He did at the close, it would be the last humiliation for Eliphaz to find that after all, from God's standpoint, Job was the only one among them who was right. In the meantime it is far easier to stand by the utterances of Eliphaz than by the utterances of Job.

The Pharisee is an intense moralist (see John 16:2; Hebrews 13:13). When Jesus Christ came He was found to be unresolvable by every set of religious principles, that was His "reproach." To "go forth therefore unto him without the camp, bearing his reproach" (Hebrews 13:13) does not mean going outside the worldly crowd; it means being put outside the religious crowd you belong to. One of the most poignant bits of suffering for a disciple comes along that line. If you remain true to Jesus Christ there are times when you will have to go through your convictions and out the other side, and most of us shrink from such a step because it means going alone. The "camp" means the religious set you belong to; the set you do not belong to does not matter to you.

Eliphaz is certain that Job is so bad that he wonders at the patience of God with him. If Eliphaz had been in the position of God, he would have excommunicated Job right away; and yet Job is the one who is face to face with reality. Today men are not asking, "Is the thing true?" but "Is it real?" It is a matter of indifference whether a thing is true; any number of things can be demonstrated to be true which do not matter to us. Have I a real God, or am I trying to produce a Pharisaic cloak for myself? Job would not accept a Pharisaic cloak; he would not grant that he was wrong, neither would he say that the friends' creed was right. He was in a quandary, but he knew that God was real, and therefore he would wait until He appeared.

The Revolutionary Struggle of Prayer (Job 23–24)

Oh that I knew where I might find him! that I might come even to his seat! I would order my cause before him, and fill my mouth with arguments. (23:3–4)

There is no reality without struggling. If you are not called to wrestle, it is only because the wrestling is being done for you.
             —DR. FORSYTH

The reason the experience of redemption is so easy is because it cost God so much. If my religion slips easily into my life it is because someone else has paid the price for it. If, however, the simple experience is taken as true to the whole of life, we will be misled; only if we take the experience of those who have paid the price for us, do we get to reality. It is men like Job and the apostle Paul who bring us to the basis of things, not the average Christian among us, who knows no more why the basis of his salvation is redemption than the average common-sense man knows the basis of ordinary human life. We must get hold of the great souls, the men who have been hard hit and have gone to the basis of things, and whose experiences have been preserved for us by God, that we may know where we stand.

One of the reasons for the futility of pseudo-evangelism is that it bases its doctrine on the shallow weak things it has saved. Thank God, Christianity does save the shallow weak things, but they are not the ones to diagnose Christianity, they are the expression of the last reach of Christianity. Paul said—". . . not many mighty, not many noble, are called" (1 Corinthians 1:26)—he did not say "not *any* mighty, not *any* noble." It is our Lord Himself, and men like Job in the Old Testament and Paul in the New who give us the indication of where we are to look for the foundation of our faith when it is being shaken.

Job's cry, "Oh that I knew where I might find him" (Job 23:3) is the birth of evangelical prayer on the basis of redemption. The "finding" cannot be by reasoning or by religious faith; the only way to find God is through prayer. In the religious life of the Pharisee, prayer becomes a rite, a ceremony. In all religion based on sound principles prayer is an exercise, a ceremony, it is not blood or passion, not actual from the whole manhood. In such prayers there is magnificently beautiful diction which one needs to be in a calm, quiet state of mind to appreciate. The most beautiful prayers are prayers that are rites, but they are apt to be mere repetition, and not of the nature of reality. There is no sting in them, no tremendous grip of a man face to face with things. There is no way out by rites or by religious beliefs, but only, as Jesus Christ indicates, by prayer.

It takes a tremendous amount of reiteration on God's part before we understand what prayer is. We do not pray at all until we are at our wits' end. ". . . their soul fainted in them. *Then* they cried unto the LORD in their trouble" (Psalm 107:5–6). During this war many a man has prayed for the first time in his life. When a man is at his wits' end it is not a cowardly thing to pray, it is the only way he can get in touch with reality. "Oh that I knew where I could get into touch with the reality that explains things!" There is only one way, and that is the way of prayer (see 1 John 5:14–15).

There are undoubtedly things which present a puzzle, e.g., the presentation of the basis of redemption; how am I going to understand whether the redemption covers everything, or only partially covers? Never by reasoning, only by prayer; and as sure as God is God you will get the answer and know of a certainty. If we take the line of disputing and spitting fire like Eliphaz did, we will get at nothing. We do not get insight by struggling, but by going to God in prayer. Most of us are wise in our own conceits, we have notions of our own which we want to see through. There is nothing to be valued more highly than to have people praying for us; God links up His power in answer to their prayers.

Redemption is easy to experience because it cost God everything, and if I am going to be regenerated it is going to cost me something. I have to give up my right to myself. I have deliberately to accept into myself something that will fight for all it is worth, something that will war against the desires of the flesh, and that will ask me to go into identification with the death of Jesus Christ, and these things produce a struggle in me. The majority of us prefer to get up and ride rather than to "get out and shove." It is only the people who "get out and shove" who really make things go. The men who are up against things just now and who are determined to get at reality at all costs, and will not accept a thing on the religious line unless that line states reality—these are the men who are paying the price for the next generation. The reason we are here in the natural world is because our mothers struggled for our existence, and the more unhindered the birth pangs the stronger and healthier the child. A thing is worth just what it costs.

The Redundant Noise of Position (Job 25)

Then answered Bildad the Shuhite, and said, Dominion and fear are with him, he maketh peace in his high places. Is there any number of his armies? and upon whom doth not his light arise? (vv. 1–3)

We have the modern and insidious type of Pharisaism, the unconscious hypocrite, the man or woman not of fraud, but of pose, not of deep and dark design, but of subtle egotism, prompt certainty and facile religiosity.

—Dr. Forsyth

Bildad's utterances here are inadvertent and wildly away from the theme. The modern Pharisee of the "Bildad" type is the man who has a pose to keep up; he is not touched by any problem himself, and when there is trouble he comes out with these redundant phrases. Job does not get annoyed with Bildad, he is rather full of pity for him. Eliphaz stings Job because he takes up a superior position; he knows why Job suffers; he stands strong for his set of principles, but he is not in touch with reality. Bildad is in touch with nothing, he is courageously heartless; he never thinks when he talks, but simply pours it out. The "Bildad" type is often met with in the pulpit; men roll out phrases and talk the most ponderous stuff with nothing in it. It is like a roll of thunder over your head when what you want is real nourishment. These men continually brought things to the surface and said to Job, "This is what you want."

What a man wants is somewhere to rest his mind and heart, and the only place to rest in is God, and the only way to come to God is by prayer. Much of our praying has nothing in it; it is not the talk of a child to his Father when he has come up against things or is hurt. "Ask, and it shall be given you," Jesus says (Luke 11:9). We do not ask, we worry, whereas one minute in prayer will put God's decree at work, namely, that He answers prayer on the ground of redemption. Jesus Christ did not say, "Ask what you like, and it shall be done unto you," but "ask what you will, ask when your will is in the thing that is a real problem to you," and God has pledged His honor that you will get the answer every time.

Parables

Be near me when my light is low,
When the blood creeps, and the nerves prick
And tingle; and the heart is sick,
And all the wheels of Being slow.

Be near me when the sensuous frame
Is rack'd with pangs that conquer trust;
And Time, a maniac scattering dust,
And Life, a Fury slinging flame.

Be near me when my faith is dry,
And men the flies of latter spring,
That lay their eggs, and sting and sing
And weave their petty cells and die.

Be near me when I fade away,
To point the term of human strife.
And on the low dark verge of life
The twilight of eternal day.

—TENNYSON

A parable is an earthly story which does not explain itself. Every one of us has an earthly story and the explanation of it is not to be found in its own expression, but only in the domain of the designer of life. Job says that the explanation his friends give of his earthly story is hopeless, they are nowhere near understanding it; God alone is the source from whence will come the explanation of all he is going through.

God and the Sublimities (Job 26)

Lo, these are parts of his ways: but how little a portion is heard of him? but the thunder of his power who can understand? (v. 14)

The sublime things in nature swamp our intelligent understanding of them; rugged mountain scenery, for instance, will awaken a sense of the sublime. The man who has never had the sense of the sublime awakened in him is scarcely born. The story of the earth itself is so full of sublimities that it requires God, not man, to expound it. If a man cannot expound the sublimities of nature, he need not expect to be able to expound the sublimity of the human soul. The sublimities of nature cannot be explained on the line of reason, but only on the line of the a-logical, that which goes beyond and underneath the logical. Job recognizes this, and he implies, "If you imagine you can explain the deeper sublimities of a man's soul, you have not pondered human life enough." The Psalmist puts it in this way—"My God, Thou art the God of the mountains and of the fathomless deep, the God of the early mornings and late at nights; but there are deeper depths than these in me, my God; more mysterious things in my soul, and I cannot fathom my own way, therefore search me, O God" (see Psalm 139). Job is on the same line.

"Lo, these are but the outskirts of his ways: and how small a whisper do we hear of him!" (see Job 26:14). In the book of Job nature is always referred to as being wild; this is a point of view we have forgotten nowadays. We talk about laws and findings, we give scientific explanations of thunder and of a sunset, and come to the conclusion that there is no unexplained sublimity in nature at all. The wildness of nature has to be recognized, there are forces in the earth and air and sea which baffle attempts at explanation or of control; all we can do is to give a direction for thought along certain lines.

Neither logic nor science can explain the sublimities of nature. Supposing a scientist with a diseased olfactory nerve says that there is no perfume in a rose, and to prove his statement he dissects the rose and tabulates every part, and then says, "Where is the perfume? It is a fiction; I have demonstrated that there is none." There is always one fact more that science cannot explain, and the best thing to do is not to deny it in order to preserve your sanity, but to say, as Job did, "No, the one fact more which you cannot explain means that God must step in just there, or there is no explanation to be had."

God and the Subtleties (Job 27)

Moreover Job continued his parable, and said, God forbid that I should justify you: till I die I will not remove mine integrity from me. My righteousness I hold fast, and will not let it go: my heart shall not reproach me so long as I live. (vv. 1, 5–6)

God is never subtle in His revelations, but always elemental and simple. The "simple Gospel" does not mean simple to understand, but simple in the way God Himself is simple. Job says, "I have no explanation as yet of what I am going through; your explanation on the line of your creed is irritating nonsense, because it makes you leave out the facts which I know, while you try to explain the One none of us can get at, namely, God." Job is not speaking in spite, but in honesty—"If I were to justify you in your explanation I should sin against my conscience, and say that you have told the truth whereas in reality you have told a lie."

There is a difference between the subtlety of Eliphaz and the subtlety of Job. Eliphaz sums up the history of the wicked man and says that God does all these things to punish him, whereas Job recognizes that the history of any man cannot be accounted for on the surface, and that God alone can explain His own dealings. The description Elpihaz gives of the wicked man is a covert condemnation of Job; he takes the facts of Job's present condition and puts them as the picture of a wicked man, while all the time he implies, "Thou art the man" (2 Samuel 12:7). "That is not the way to comfort me, or bring me any help," says Job. He does not brag and say he is a good man, but he does maintain that the reason he suffers is not because he is bad. "You pretend to know the attitude of God to things, but all that you describe as the experience of a wicked man I can give as my experience of being a good man."

The explanation of Job's suffering is the fact that God and Satan had made a battleground of his soul. It was not for Job's chastening or his perfecting, but for an ulterior purpose which he did not know, but his intuition made him stick to the fact that the only One who could explain the sublimities of nature was the One who could explain what he was going through. "Though he slay me" (Job 13:15), though my creed goes and everything is destroyed, "yet I will trust in him"—not trust Him to deliver me, but trust that He is honorable and just and true, and that I shall yet be justified in sticking to my faith in His honor, though meantime it looks as if He is deliberately destroying me.

There is a lot of cheap talk just now regarding the British Empire and how God is punishing us for our sins—a hopeless misrepresentation. The cross of Calvary and the redemption have to do with the sins of the world. If God began to punish the nations for their sins there would be no nation left on the face of the earth. Job takes the right line, that the difficulties are produced by a conflict of wills.

Beware of the subtleties which twist facts. It is possible to torture a man with a delicate type of mind, as in the case of Ugo Bassi[20], torture him not physically, but by suggesting that he has been guilty of base motives and deeds. The sensitiveness of Ugo Bassi's mind was such that after a while he began to believe he had been guilty unconsciously of the things he was accused of. Job's friends said to him, "We have all these facts about you, and they are only explainable along the line that you are a bad man; you may not be conscious of your badness, nevertheless you are a hypocrite, because our creed says that if a man trusts God, God will bless him; and instead of being blessed, you have been cursed in every way and have lost everything: therefore you must be a bad man." If Job had been of the Ugo Bassi stamp with a hypersensitive mind and not the robust spirit he was, he would have said, "Oh, well, I must be much worse than I imagined; and I must be guilty." But he stuck to it, "No, I have not been dishonorable and bad, you may say of me what you like, but that is not the reason why I suffer."

God and the Terrestrial World (Job 28)

Surely there is a vein for the silver, and a place for gold where they fine it. Iron is taken out of the earth, and brass is molten out of the stone. (vv. 1–2)

Careful examination of every reference Job makes to geology or meteorology reveals that there is no significant or insignificant blunder in all he says; every reference is a piece of consummate accuracy. This is passing.

Every common-sense fact requires something for its explanation which common sense cannot give. The facts of every day and night reveal things our own minds cannot explain. When a scientific man comes across a gap in his explanations, instead of saying, "There is no gap here," let him recognize that there is a gap he cannot bridge, and that he must be reverent with what he cannot understand. The tendency is to deny that a fact has any existence because it cannot be fitted into any explanation as yet. That "the exception proves the rule" is not true: the exception proves that the rule won't do; the rule is only useful in the greatest number of cases.

When scientists treat a thesis as a fact they mean that it is based on the highest degree of probability. There are no "infallible" findings, and the man who bows down to scientific findings may be as big a fool as the man who refuses to do so. The man who prays ceases to be a fool, while the man who refuses to pray nourishes a blind life within his own brain and he will find no way out on that road. Job cries out that prayer is the only way out in all these matters—

Whence then cometh wisdom? and where is the place of understanding? Behold, the fear of the LORD, that is wisdom: and to depart from evil is understanding. (vv. 20, 28)

God and the Shadows (Job 29)

Oh that I were as in months past, as in the days when God preserved me; when his candle shined upon my head, and when by his light I walked through darkness. (vv. 2–3)

> *Truth for ever on the scaffold,*
> *Wrong for ever on the throne,—*

Yet that scaffold sways the future,
and, behind the dim unknown.
Standeth God within the shadow,
keeping watch above his own.

—JAMES RUSSELL HOWELL

The "shadows" depict what Job is describing, namely, the things in human history and in personal experience that are shadowed by mystery and cannot be explained by reason or religious creeds, but only by belief in God who will make all plain in His own way. Job is saying that there is nothing in life you can reckon on with any certainty. We may say that if a man has been well brought up and has developed his own integrity and lived rightly, success will be sure to attend him, but you cannot calculate along that line.

Never ignore the things that cannot be explained, put them on one side, but remember they are there and have to be reckoned with. There is a gap and a wildness in things and if God does not step in and adjust it, there is no hope; but God has stepped in by the redemption, and our part is to trust confidently in Him. Either the pessimist is right when he says we are autumn leaves driven by the blast of some ultimate power without mind, or else the way out is by the redemption of Jesus Christ.

God and the Obscene (Job 30)

And now I am their song, yea, I am their byword. . . . They flee far from me, and spare not to spit in my face. (vv. 9–10)

Jesus Christ was in the case Job is describing, He was placed alongside the most obscene immorality of His day—"Behold, a gluttonous man, and a winebibber, a friend of publicans and sinners!" (Luke 7:34). And He was put to death between two malefactors. It is impossible to calculate on the line that virtue will bring a man to honor, and that uprightness will escape the punishment which falls on men who are not upright. Any explanation at all leaves a gap which cannot be bridged as yet.

God and the Scrupulous (Job 31)

If I have walked with vanity, or if my foot hath hasted to deceit; let me be weighed in an even balance that God may know mine integrity. (vv. 5–6)

Job examines the statements of the creed and its moral findings, and then disputes it from his own experience—"Do you think I am trying to make out before God that I am what I have not been? would I talk to God with what would be blatant insolence if I had not the facts to back me up? The inference from the facts of my life is that I have been beyond reproach, and in my approach to God I will not say I have been guilty of what I know I have not been. I stand clear before God on every one of these lines, and though I do not see Him or know Him, I will stick to it that He is other than you say, and that when I do see Him He will not say that I deceived myself when I spoke the truth."

It is foolish to say that this chapter refers to a past dispensation and that we are in advance of it. We are in another dispensation, but not necessarily a better one. What man among us can come anywhere near the standard of integrity of Job? That kind of statement comes from accepting principles for guidance instead of a personal relationship. If I worship God from fear or superstition, then I am wrong, my heart has been "secretly enticed" (Job 31:27). Job's point of view is that if I do anything in order to

appease God, I am committing iniquity. The only reason for my
approach to God must be that He is what I believe Him to be, a
God of honor and justice, not a God of manipulative magic who
demands that we do things without any reason. Today we are
dealing with the very thing for which the friends have pulled Job
to pieces. There are people who say, "I will not, I dare not, accept
the God you are presenting because He is not a moral God; there
is something wrong in such a presentation, my whole being cries
out against it, I cannot go to such a God as a deliverer."

In these chapters Job is insisting that God must be other
than his former creed said He was, and that it must be acknowledged that there are facts which the creed had not taken into
account. Thank God for theology, but theology is second, not
first; if we put it first, we will do what the friends did, refuse to
look at facts and remain consistent to certain ideas which pervert
the character of God. In the final run God will not have us say
an untrue thing for the sake of His honor.

The Passion for Authority

JOB 32–37

In Elihu the passion for authority is represented. The average man in Job's condition is apt to break away from all authority. A lesser man than Job would have become a philosopher and said that every man is a law unto himself, i.e., his own inner consciousness is sufficient law. Job was not of this order, neither was Elihu. The passion for authority is a noble one, but Elihu missed out on the fact that authority to be worthy arises out of the nature of a superior moral integrity, and not simply from one who happens to be higher up in the scale than ourselves.

Elihu comes with the idea that because God has said a thing, therefore it is authoritative: Job wants to know what kind of God it was who said it, is He a being whose character does not contradict the moral basis of life? Authority must be of a moral, not a superstitious character. Elihu's contention is, "Because God has said so," that is sufficient; or, "Because the creed says so," therefore it must be blindly accepted. To be without any authority is to be lawless, but to have only an internal authority is as bad as having a blind external authority; the two must meet together somehow.

The Inspiration of Autocratic Authority (Job 32)

Autocratic authority means to rule by right of insistence, not necessarily by right of personal integrity. Napoleon said of Jesus

Christ that He had succeeded in making every human soul an appendage of His own because He had the genius of holiness. Other men exercised authority by coercive means, Jesus Christ never did, His authority was *worthy*. He proved Himself worthy not only in the domain of God, which we do not know, but in the domain of man, which we do know; He is worthy there, consequently He prevails to open the book (see Revelation 5). Authority to be lasting must be of the same order as that of Jesus Christ, not the authority of autocracy or coercion, but the authority of worth, to which all that is worthy in a man bows down. It is only the unworthy in a man that does not bow down to worthy authority.

The Superior Conceit of Shyness (Job 32:1–22)

And Elihu the son of Barachel the Buzite answered and said, I am young, and ye are very old; wherefore I was afraid, and durst not shew you mine opinion. Behold, I waited for your words; I gave ear to your reasons, while ye searched out what to say. Yea, I attended unto you, and behold, there was none of you that convinced Job, or that answered his words. (vv. 6, 11–12)

There is a fine apparent modesty about Elihu. He says, "I waited for you to speak, but all I have listened to has made me angry, because Job has justified himself at the expense of God, and you have stopped short without challenging him in the right way, and now I will speak."

Then was kindled the wrath of Elihu . . . against Job was his wrath kindled, because he justified himself rather than God. (v. 2)

Elihu exhibits the superior conceit of shyness. There is quite possibly a superior conceit in a shy or quiet man. A man may keep silent not because he is really modest, but he does not intend to speak until he gets a proper audience—"I do not intend to bring out my notion of things until people are prepared to listen; I do not wish what I say to go into the mere rush of ordinary conversation, so I shall wait for a suitable opportunity." This does not altogether diagnose Elihu, but he certainly exhibits this characteristic.

Elihu says that the inspiration of authority comes from God simply because He is God, and not from any sense of right in Himself. Job stands up against this; he says, in effect, "I will not accept any authority on the ground of superstition; I must know the moral ingredient in the authority." This is the element Elihu loses sight of altogether.

The Insistence of Autocratic Authority (Job 33)

The Spiritual Consciousness of Submission (Job 33:1-22)

Behold, in this thou art not just: I will answer thee, that God is greater than man. Why dost thou strive against him? for he giveth not account of any of his matters. (vv. 12–13)

The antagonism of the friends in battling for their creed was an indication that they were getting shaky regarding it. But Elihu is not shaky, he does not accept the creed of the other three, he has a notion of his own based on the conception of autocratic authority, namely, that no man has any right to inquire whether God is good; it is a question of His supreme authority, and submission is the only line to take. It is dangerous to be conscious of submission to a spiritual power. The difference between fatalism and faith lies just here. Fatalism means, "My number's up; I have to bow to the power whether I like it or not; I do not know the character of the power, but it is greater than I am, and I must submit." The submission of faith is that I do know the character of the power, and this was the line Job took— "Though He slay me, yet I will trust the fact that His character is worthy." This is the attitude of faith all through—"I submit to One whose character I know but whose ways are obscured in mystery just now."

We do know the character of God, if we are Christians, because we have it revealed to us in Jesus Christ—"He that hath seen me hath seen the Father" (John 14:9). Anything that contradicts the manifestation given in and through the Lord Jesus Christ cannot be true of God. Therefore we know that the character of God is noble and true and right, and any authority from God is based, not on autocracy or mere blind power, but on worthiness which everything in me recognizes as worthy, therefore I submit. Elihu was moved with indignation because Job said, "I cannot submit to the fact that God has decreed such things as you say; you must give me room to say that your credal exposition of God is wrong. By your creed you prove me to be wrong where I know I am right; therefore if the facts I do know are disproved by you, how can I accept your explanation of the facts I do not know?" Elihu says God does not explain Himself, and you have no right to try and find Him out, it is sufficient to know that the autocratic authority of the Omnipotent has spoken, therefore you must submit. Job's sufferings have produced in him this attitude—"I want to know where what you call the supreme authority of the Almighty gets a hold on the moral line of things, where it agrees, in part at least, with what I understand as worthy."

The same thing occurs in matters of religious controversy. Am I going to submit to the authority of a church, or a book or to the authority of a person? If I submit to the authority of a person it must be demonstrated that that person is greater than I am on the "worthy" line, the line which is recognized as worthy by the majority of sane humanity; if He is greater there, then I will bow down to His authority at once.

The Indictment of Autobiographic Antagonism (Job 34–35)

The Suffering Chastisement of Sinfulness (Job 34:35–37)

Job hath spoken without knowledge, and his words were without wisdom. My desire is that Job may be tried unto the end because of his answers for wicked men. For he addeth rebellion unto his sin, he clappeth his hands among us, and multiplieth his words against God.

Elihu sums up the autobiographic side, the subjective side. The great phase at present is the sophisticated conception that a man is a law unto himself. Elihu is in advance of that: he says there is an authority other than myself. Job is looking for an authority, and he gives his own subjective experiences as the reason for disbelieving the presentation of God which has been given. On the ground of what he was going through, he was indignant at this presentation. Elihu says, "Your experiences are explainable on the line that you are a sinful man, not a hypocrite, as the others have said, but sinful, and God is chastising you. You have spoken rashly and wildly, and this is the way God is answering." This kind of view presents a conception not really based on facts, but which easily melts down any opposition by its sentimental presentation.

The Sentimental Conception of the
Supreme (Job 35:10–11)

*But none saith, Where is God my maker, who giveth songs
in the night; who teacheth us more than the beasts of the
earth, and maketh us wiser than the fowls of the heaven?*

There is no pretense about Elihu; he says some sublime
things, but in his tirade against experience he introduces a line
that stirs up human sympathies without the basis of facts underneath. The sentimental line stirs up a conception of things which
overlooks both the actual and the real facts and sweeps a man off
his feet. It is all very well to have experiences, but there must be
a standard for measuring them, and a standard more worthy
than my own on the line on which I know I am worthy. The
standard for Christian experience is not the experience of another
Christian, but God Himself. "Be ye therefore perfect, even as
your Father which is in heaven is perfect" (Matthew 5:48). "If
you are my disciple," says Jesus, "the standard by which you are
to measure your experiences as a regenerated saint is the character of God." "They took knowledge of them, that they had been
with Jesus" (Acts 4:13). The apostles bore a strong family likeness to Jesus Christ, their experience and their character were
being brought up to God's standard.

There must be an authority which is internal as well as external. The tendency nowadays is to have no authority at all. A man
says, "I will have no Church, no Bible, no God, nothing but my
own self-realization." This is the modern phase of sophisticated
religion. Every bit of morality a man has demands that there
should be, not a coercive or autocratic authority, but a worthy
authority. Elihu is speaking to Job on the subjective line as
though Job were saying that there was no authority whatever

binding upon him; whereas Job is getting at the right relationship to the real standard, and his protest is against a presentation of the standard which is not worthy.

The Interpretation of Absolute Authority (Job 36–37)

Elihu also proceeded, and said, Suffer me a little, and I will shew thee that I have yet to speak on God's behalf. (36:1–2)

If one may say it reverently, Almighty God is nothing but a mental abstraction unless He becomes concrete and actual, because an ideal has no power unless it can be realized. The doctrine of the incarnation is that God did become actual, He manifested Himself on the plane of human flesh, and "Jesus Christ" is the name not only for God and man in one, but the name of the personal Savior who makes the way back for every man to get into a personal relationship with God. Jesus Christ declares that He is the exclusive way to the Father— ". . . neither knoweth any man the Father, save the Son, and he to whomsoever the Son will reveal him" (Matthew 11:27). Any theology which ignores Jesus Christ as the supreme authority ceases to be Christian theology. "I am the way" (John 14:6), said Jesus, not the road we leave behind us, but the way we stay in: "no man cometh unto the Father, but by me." On the ground of His absolute, not coercive, authority, every man recognizes sooner or later that Jesus Christ stands easily first.

The Supreme Character of the Sublime (Job 36:22–26)

Behold, God exalteth by his power: who teacheth like him? (v. 22)

Job's contention is that he has proved by experience that what he has been told about God cannot be true, "because," he says, "when you try to explain the facts I know in the light of the one whom you call God, you have to deny those facts; therefore I must conclude that your exposition of God is wrong." Elihu goes back to the position that it is no use trying to find out whether God is worthy; it is sufficient to know that He is supreme, a being who issues His orders without the remotest regard to moral right; and the man who dares to try and discover whether the authority of God is morally right is a blasphemer and a dangerous man. Voltaire's talk about God was mainly tremendous indignation at the presentation of God then prevailing.

There is always a tendency to produce an absolute authority; we accept the authority of the church, or of the Bible, or of a creed, and often refuse to do any more thinking on the matter; and in so doing we ignore the essential nature of Christianity which is based on a personal relationship to Jesus Christ, and works on the basis of our responsibility. On the ground of the redemption I am saved and God puts His Holy Spirit into me, then He expects me to react on the basis of that relationship. I can evade it by dumping my responsibility on to a church, or a book or a creed, forgetting what Jesus said—"Search the scriptures, for in them ye think ye have eternal life; and they are they which testify of me; and ye will not come to me, that ye might have life" (John 5:39–40). The only way to understand the Scriptures is not to accept them blindly, but to read them in the light of a personal relationship to Jesus Christ.

If we insist that a man must believe the doctrine of the Trinity and the inspiration of the Scriptures before he can be saved, we are putting the cart before the horse. All that is the effect of being a Christian, not the cause of it; and if we put the effect first we produce difficulties because we are putting thinking before life. Jesus says, "Come unto me" (Matthew 11:28), and if you want to know whether My teaching is of God, do His will. A scientist can explain the universe in which common-sense men live, but the scientific explanation is not first; life is first. The same with theology; theology is the systematizing of the intellectual expression of life from God; it is a mighty thing, but it is second, not first.

The Sorrowful Condemnation of Sanity (Job 37:23–24)

Touching the Almighty, we cannot find him out: he is excellent in power, and in judgment, and in plenty of justice; he will not afflict. Men do therefore fear him: he respecteth not any that are wise of heart.

Elihu condemns Job sorrowfully, but absolutely; he declares that not only has Job made shipwreck of his faith, but he has become defiant in silencing the friends.

Job will not accept anything blindly, he says, "I must see that it does not contradict what I know." The apostle Paul speaks of "the foolishness of God" (1 Corinthians 1:25) as pitted against the wisdom of men, and the wisdom of men when it saw Jesus Christ said, "That cannot be God." When the Judaic ritualists saw Jesus Christ, they said, "You are a blasphemer; You do not express God at all." Anna and Simeon were the only two of the descendants of Abraham who recognized who Jesus was, hence the condemnation of the other crowd. If two who had lived a life of communion with God could detect Jehovah as the babe of Bethlehem within the symbolism, the others who did not recognize Him are to be condemned. They did not see Him because they had become blinded on the line of absolute authority, the line of symbolism or creed, and when that which was symbolized appeared, they could not see Him.

Every phase of this book, with the exception of Job's own utterances, takes up the challenge of Satan—"No man, no matter how good he is, loves You for Your own sake. You call Job perfect, but touch the things You have given him, destroy his blessings, and he will curse You to Your face." Job's blessings were destroyed, and yet he clings to it, "I don't know the reason why I suffer; the reason you give is not the one. God alone can explain it to me, and I will wait for Him." Part of the gamble was that God must keep out of sight, and that Job must not be aided, and he was not. The exposition of Job's sufferings must be given in the light of this preface, which was never made known to him. Job never knew that Satan and Jehovah had made a battleground of his soul.

The problem in the book of Job represents the problem of the whole world. No matter what a man's experiences may be, whether slight or terrific, there is something in this book which gives him an indication as to why the redemption was necessary, and also a line of explaining the otherwise inexplicable things of human experience.

The Passion for Reality

We cannot kindle when we will
The fire which in the heart resides;
The spirit bloweth and is still,
In mystery our soul abides.
   But tasks in hours of insight will'd
   Can be through hours of gloom fulfill'd
With aching hands and bleeding feet
We dig and heap, lay stone on stone;
We bear the burden and the heat
Of the long day, and wish 'twere done,
   Not till the hours of light return.
   All we have built do we discern.

—MATTHEW ARNOLD[21]

The word "reality" is used to represent the realm of God and the whole of mankind in correspondence. The creeds give us a theological statement of God, but Job's experience proves that a statement of belief does not give us God. The only way we get at God is through conscience, because through conscience we get at the moral relation to things. We have seen that Job would not bow down to an authority which had not its basis in what was right in actual life. God has to clear Himself from the wrong presentation given of Him by the friends, and although Job is right in repudiating their presentation, God rebukes him for remaining too much of an agnostic, and He leads him out along the line indicated when he said, "Though he slay me, yet will I trust in him" (Job 13:15), i.e., "I will trust that God is what my innate manhood tells me He must be." The authority we blindly grope after is God Himself, not a tendency making for righteousness, not a set of principles. Behind reality is God Himself, and the final authority is a personal relationship. Christianity is a personal relationship to a personal God on the ground of the redemption. The reason Jesus Christ is our Lord and Master is not first because He is God incarnate, but because He is easily first in the human domain.

The Still Small Voice of God (Job 38:1–4a)

Then the LORD answered Job out of the whirlwind, and said, Who is this that darkeneth counsel by words without knowledge? Gird up now thy loins like a man; for I will demand of thee, and answer thou me. Where wast thou when I laid the foundations of the earth? . . . (see also 40:6–7)

God arraigns both Elihu and Job, He appeals to them to come before Him on the basis of their actual knowledge, and while being true to the facts they know, to leave room for facts they do not know. The "still small voice" (1 Kings 19:12) is an appeal not to a superstitious belief in God, but to the actuality of God to man. God disposes altogether of a relationship to Himself born of superstitious dread—"No, stand like a man, and listen to facts as they are." God counsels Job—"Don't come to too hasty a conclusion, but gird up your loins like a man and wait. You have done right so far in that you would not have Me misrepresented, but you must recognize that there are facts you do not know, and wait for Me to give the revelation of them on the ground of your moral obedience." Job would not bow before God on the basis of superstition; he could not conceive such a God to be worthy. The ground of appeal is not that God says I must do a certain thing, but that the manhood in me recognizes that what God says is likely to be right. Jesus Christ never coerced anyone; He never used the apparatus of the priestly or of super-natural powers, or what we understand by revivals; He faced men on the ground on which all men stood, and refused to stag-ger human wits into submission to Himself.

The Sub-Scientific Value of Immanence
(Job 38:4b–41)

"Immanence" means the notion of the immediate presence of God pervading everything, and the pantheist says that this view explains everything. Elihu is stating with enormous airs that "humanity" is another name for God; whereas one of the big Bible doctrines is that humanity is not God, and was created to be distinctly not God. There is evidence that God is in the facts of nature, but also evidence that He is other than nature. We may make a working definition of the laws of nature, "but, remember," says God, "behind those laws I come."

Scientific dogmatism is as dangerous as religious dogmatism. Religious dogmatism takes a man's experience and tells him why everything has happened; but every now and again things hap-pen outside human experience which cannot be explained. It is well to note what can be known, but no one has any right to be dogmatic about the things which cannot be known saving by revelation. We can state scientific laws so far as we have been able to discover them, but we are outside our domain if we say that those laws govern regions we know nothing about. Inferences based on the facts I know will never enable me to find God. I may study all the facts of geology and natural history, but where does the note of authority come in it all? The note of authority comes only through conscience. Laws are effects, not causes. If we can know God by means of our intellect, then Jesus Christ's claim to reveal God is a farce, and the redemption nonsense.

Job declared that he could not know God—"I do not know God," he says, "but I do know that the God you describe in your creed cannot be God, because in order to make Him God you have to deny facts which I know." The friends said that the way out was to accept the agnostic position and become a fatalist— "Don't try to find out whether God's character is noble and right," and they ended in telling an untruth about God. God says, "When I reveal Myself it will be as the God of the morality you know," and yet we must never tie God up along the line of subjective experience.

The only reality in life is moral reality, not intellectual or aesthetic. Religion based on intellectualism becomes purely credal, Jesus Christ is not needed in it. The intellect does not get us at reality, neither do the emotions alone, but conscience does, as soon as it relates itself to these two. The basis of things is not rational. Reason and intellect are our guides among things as they are, but they cannot explain things as they are. For instance, it is not rational that Christian nations should be at war. The basis of things is tragic, and intellect makes a man shut his eyes to this fact and become a superior person. One of the great crimes of intellectual philosophy is that it destroys a man as a human being and turns him into a supercilious spectator; he cuts himself off from relationship with human stuff as it is and becomes a statue.

A moral man, i.e., the man who will do the right and be the right thing in actual life, is more likely than any other kind of man to recognize God when He manifests Himself. If I become a devotee of a creed I cannot see God unless He comes along my line. It takes the whole man—conscience, intellect, will and emotions, to discover God as reality. The man who is standing well within his own right, whose conscience is not yet awakened, feels no need of God. "I did not come to call him," said Jesus. But let a man come up against things, and he will find not a creed or a doctrine, but the reality of God. The elemental facts a man comes up against transform his stubbornness into amenableness to reality.

The Supernormal Vindication of Morality
(Job 39–41)

Wilt thou also disannul my judgment? wilt thou condemn me that thou mayest be righteous? (40:8)

In these chapters the whole of the universe is symbolized, and whatever the universe is, it is not tame. A certain type of modern science would have us believe it is, that we can harness the sea and air and earth. Quite true, you can, if you only read scientific manuals and deal with successful experiments; but before long you discover elements which knock all your calculations on the head and prove that the universe is wild and unmanageable. And yet in the beginning God intended man to control it; the reason he cannot is because he twisted God's order; instead of recognizing God's dominion over himself, man became his own god, and by so doing lost control of everything else (see Genesis 3).

When Jesus Christ came He was easily master of the life in the air and earth and sky, and in Him we see the order God originally intended for man. If you want to know what the human race is to be like on the basis of the redemption, you will find it mirrored in Jesus Christ—a perfect oneness between God and man, no gap; in the meantime there is a gap, and the universe is wild, not tame. Every type of superstition pretends it can rule the universe, the scientific quack proclaims he can control the weather, that he has occult powers and can take the untameable universe and tame it. God says it cannot be done.

The Strangely Stirred Valley of Job (Job 40)

Then Job answered the LORD, *and said, Behold I am vile; what shall I answer thee? I will lay mine hand upon my mouth. Once have I spoken; but I will not answer: yea, twice; but I will proceed no further. (vv. 3–5)*

There is nothing cringing in Job's attitude, it is the bowing down of a man strangely stirred in humiliation by the realization that he is face to face with that which is superior to himself.

The revelation given by Jesus Christ of God is not the revelation of Almighty God, but of the essential nature of deity—unutterable humility and moral purity, utterly worthy in every detail of actual life. In the incarnation God proves Himself worthy in the sphere in which we live, and this is the sphere of the revelation of the self-giving of God. Job recognizes this; he knows it is no superstition-monger, or creed-monger, or theology-monger, speaking to him, but the voice of God, because this voice does not contradict what he knows, but leads him straight out to what he could never discover for himself. And so Job bows his head in true humility before God and listens—"I am on the right track at last."

Locks vs. Keys

JOB 42:1–6

You tell me, doubt is Devil-born
I know not: one indeed I knew
In many a subtle question versed,
Who touch'd a jarring lyre first,
But ever strove to make it true:

Perplext in faith, but pure in deeds,
At last he beat his music out.
There lives more faith in honest doubt,
Believe me, than in half the creeds.

He fought his doubts and gather'd strength
He would not make his judgment blind.
He faced the spectres of the mind
And laid them: thus he came at length

To find a stronger faith his own;
And Power was with him in the night,
Which makes the darkness and the light,
And dwells not in the light alone,

But in the darkness and the cloud,
As over Sinai's peaks of old,
While Israel made their gods of gold,
Altho' the trumpet blew so loud.

—Tennyson

Everything a man takes to be the key to a problem is apt to turn out to be another lock. For instance, the theory of evolution was supposed to be the key to the problem of the universe, but instead it has turned out a lock. Again, the atomic theory was thought to be the key; then it was discovered that the atom itself was composed of electrons, and each electron was found to be a universe of its own, and that theory too becomes a lock and not a key. Everything that man attempts as a simplification of life, other than a personal relationship to God, turns out to be a lock, and we should be alert to recognize when a thing turns from a key to a lock. The creed Job held, which pretended to be a key to the character of God, turned out to be a lock, and Job is realizing that the only key to life is not a statement of faith in God, nor an intellectual conception of God, but a personal relationship to Him. God Himself is the key to the riddle of the universe, and the basis of things is to be found only in Him. If a man leaves out God and takes any scientific explanation as the key, he only succeeds in finding another lock.

The Rehabilitation of Faith in God (Job 42:1–2)

As the Source and Support of All Existence

Then Job answered the LORD, and said, I know that thou canst do every thing, and that no thought can be withholden from thee.

To rehabilitate means to reinstate, to restore to former rank. The problem all through the book of Job is that the teaching of the creed and Job's implicit faith in God do not agree, and it looks as if he is a fool to hang on to his belief in God. In this last chapter we see everything rehabilitated, put back into rank, by means of Job's personal relationship to God. That is what will happen as the result of this war—many a man's faith in God will be rehabilitated. The basis of things must always be found in a personal relationship to a personal God, never in thinking or feeling.

Job says, "I cannot find any rest in your reasonings or in my own, and I refuse to avoid the facts in order to make a rational statement." Job had perfect confidence in the character of God though he did not understand the way He was taking. "Though he slay me, yet will I trust in him" (Job 13:15). We sometimes wrongly illustrate faith in God by the faith of a businessman in a check. Faith commercially is based on calculation, but religious faith cannot be illustrated by the kind of faith we exhibit in life. Faith in God is a terrific venture in the dark; I have to believe that God is good in spite of all that contradicts it in my experience. It is not easy to say that God is love (1 John 4:8) when everything that happens actually gives the lie to it. Everyone's soul represents some kind of battlefield. The point for each one is whether we will hang on, as Job did, and say "Though things look black, I will trust in God."

"Then Job *answered* the LORD. . . ." (Job 42:1). This does not mean that Job saw the Lord standing before him as a man; but that he had a trained ear as the result of his faith in God. The basis of a man's faith in God is that God is the source and support of all existence, not that He *is* all existence. Job recognizes this, and maintains that in the end everything will be explained and made clear. Have I this kind of faith—not faith in a principle, but faith *in God,* that He is just and true and right? Many of us have no faith in God at all, but only faith in what He has done for us, and when these things are not apparent we lose our faith and say, "Why should this happen to me? Why should there be a war? Why should I be wounded and sick? Why should my spouse be killed? I am going to chuck up my faith in God."

The Re-Establishment of Truth in Life and Personality (Job 42:3)

As the Source and Support of All Real Experience

Who is he that hideth counsel without knowledge? therefore have I uttered that I understood not; things too wonderful for me, which I knew not.

There is a great difference between Christian experience and Christian faith. The danger of experience is that our faith is made to rest in it, instead of seeing that our experience is simply a doorway to God Himself. The reason many of us refuse to think and discover the basis of true religion is because evangelical Christianity has been stated in such a flimsy way. We get at truth through life and personality, not by logic or scientific statements. "Therefore have I uttered that I understood not; things too wonderful for me, which I knew not." In refusing to stand by what was not true, Job uttered bigger things than he understood at the time. That is the way God uses men when they are rightly related to Him; He conveys His real presence as a sacrament through their commonplace lives. Our Lord Himself becomes real in the same way that life and personality are real. Intellect asks, "What is truth?" (John 18:38) as if truth were something that could be stated in words. "I am . . . the truth," said Jesus (John 14:6). The only way we get at truth is by life and personality. When a man is up against things it is no use for him to try and work it out logically, but let him obey, and instantly he will see his way through.

Truth is moral, not intellectual. We perceive truth by doing the right thing, not by thinking it out. "If any man will do his will, he shall know of the doctrine" (John 7:17). Men have tried to get at the truth of Christianity head-first, which is like saying you must think how you will live before you are born. We instantly see the absurdity of that, and yet we expect to reason out the Christian life before we have been born into the realm of Jesus Christ. "Except a man be born again, he cannot see the kingdom of God" (John 3:3). If ever we are to see the domain where Jesus lives and enter into it, we must be born again, become regenerated by receiving the Holy Spirit; then we shall find that truth is not in a creed or a logical statement, but in life and personality. This is what Job is realizing.

The Religious Basis of Science and Philosophy (Job 42:4)

As the Source and Support of All Abiding Exposition

Hear, I beseech thee, and I will speak: I will demand of thee, and declare thou unto me.

We are not to bring God into our system of philosophy, but to found our philosophy on God. The source and support of all abiding exposition is a man's personal relationship to God. If we base our philosophy on reason, we shall produce a false philosophy; but if we base it on faith in God, we can begin to expound life rightly. Actual conditions come into account, but underneath lies the redemption.

Sin is not man's problem, but God's. God has taken the problem of sin into His own hands and solved it, and the proof that He has is the cross of Calvary. The cross is the cross of God. On the ground of the redemption I can wash my robes, and make them "white in the blood of the Lamb" (Revelation 7:14). Pseudo-evangelism has twisted the revelation and made it mean—"Now that God has saved me, I do not need to do anything." The New Testament revelation is that now I am saved by God's grace, I must work on that basis and keep myself clean. It does not matter what a man's heredity is, or what tendencies there are in him, on the basis of the redemption he can become all that God's book indicates he should be. The essential truth of Christianity in thinking is that I can wash my robes, and make them clean in the blood of the Lamb. That is the exposition of the redemption in actual experience. Are we thinking along this line, or on the pagan line which makes out that the basis of things is rational, and leaves out God, and Jesus Christ, and the redemption altogether?

Repentance and the Dawn of God's Humanity (Job 42:5–6)

As the Source and Support of a "Second Chance"

I have heard of thee by the hearing of the ear; but now mine eye seeth thee. Wherefore I abhor myself, and repent in dust and ashes.

Because a man has altered his life it does not necessarily mean that he has repented. A man may have lived a bad life and suddenly stop being bad, not because he has repented, but because he is like an exhausted volcano. The fact that he has become good is no sign of his having become a Christian. The bedrock of Christianity is repentance. The apostle Paul never forgot what he had been; when he speaks of "forgetting those things which are behind" (Philippians 3:13), he is referring to what he has attained to; the Holy Spirit never allowed him to forget what he had been (see 1 Corinthians 15:9, Ephesians 3:8, 1 Timothy 1:13–15). Repentance means that I estimate exactly what I am in God's sight and I am sorry for it, and on the basis of the redemption I become the opposite. The only repentant man is the holy man, i.e., the one who becomes the opposite of what he was because something has entered into him. Any man who knows himself knows that he cannot be holy, therefore if he does become holy, it is because God has "shipped" something into him; he is now "presenced with divinity," and can begin to bring forth "fruits meet for repentance" (Matthew 3:8).

A man may know the plan of salvation, and preach like an archangel, and yet not be a Christian (cf. Matthew 7:21–22). The test of Christianity is that a man lives better than he preaches. The reality of the heredity of Jesus Christ comes into us through regeneration, and if ever we are to exhibit a family likeness to Him it must be because we have entered into repentance and have received something from God. If the disposition of meanness and lust and spite shows itself through my bodily life, when the disposition of Jesus Christ is there, it will show through my bodily life too, and no one need ever be afraid that he will be credited with the holiness he exhibits. "Now mine eye seeth thee," said Job. "Wherefore I abhor myself, and repent in dust and ashes" (Job 42:5–6). When I enthrone Jesus Christ I say the thing that is violently opposed to the old rule. I deny my old ways as entirely as Peter denied his Lord.

Jesus Christ's claim is that He can put a new disposition, His own disposition, Holy Spirit, into any man, and it will be manifested in all that he does. But the disposition of the Son of God can only enter my life by the way of repentance.

Disguise of the Actual

JOB 42:7–17

That low man seeks a little thing to do,
Sees it and does it:
This high man, with a great thing to pursue,
Dies ere he knows it.
That low man goes on adding one to one,
His hundred's soon hit:
This high man, aiming at a million,
Misses an unit.
That, has the world here—should he need the next
Let the world mind him!
This, throws himself on God, and unperplexed,
Seeking shall find him.

—ROBERT BROWNING

Our actual life is a disguise, no one expresses what he really is. Job could not express actually, either before or after his suffering, what he really was. The "great Divine event" to which we look forward is when the earth will actually express itself as the work of God, and saints will actually express themselves as the sons of God. Meanwhile, actual appearances do not express the real things.

All through Job has maintained his belief that God is honorable; he declares that the friends' credal statement of God was not adequate because they have said things he could disprove from his own experience. "Why I am suffering, I do not know; but your explanation does not satisfy me. Though He slay me, though I am knocked to pieces really, I believe that God is honorable, a God of love and justice, and I will wait for Him, and one day it will be proved, that my faith was right." That is the sublime reach of Job's faith. Now God takes it in hand to deal with the friends.

The Scourge of Eternal Reality (Job 42:7)

The LORD said to Eliphaz the Temanite, My wrath is kindled against thee, and against thy two friends: for ye have not spoken of me the thing that is right, as my servant Job hath.

Everyone who poses as a religious teacher is faced sooner or later by eternal reality. The friends had posed as religious teachers, they said they knew God, and their criticism of Job was along this line; but God says, "Ye have not spoken of me the thing that is right, as my servant Job hath." In reading what Job says we should probably have come to the conclusion that a man who talked as he did could not be a good man, he said such wild, extravagant things; and yet in the end God, who is eternal reality, said that he had spoken rightly of Him. A man may utter wild things which seem to us all wrong, but it will be a humiliation to find that he has spoken of God more truly than we have. When eternal reality strikes, pose is no good, religious nonsense is no good. The voice of God is scathing Eliphaz and the others, not because they had spoken untruths—they had spoken what was logically true all the time, but because they had misrepresented Him. Christianity does not consist in telling the truth, or walking in a conscientious way, or adhering to principles; Christianity is something other than all that, it is adhering in absolute surrender to a person, the Lord Jesus Christ.

If the reality of God is a scourge to a man who has never pretended to be religious, it must be ten times more so to a man who has been a religious teacher, who has said to people, "I can tell you why you suffer." "I can tell you why God has allowed this war, and what He is doing with the British Empire." When such a man comes up against eternal realities and hears God say, "You have not spoken the thing which is true of me," the scourge must be appalling (cf. John 15:2–6). Eliphaz had spoken the truth abstractly, but he had misrepresented God all through. God is not an abstract truth; He is the eternal reality, and is discerned only by means of a personal relationship.

When one is found out by eternal reality the danger is to become defiant or despairing. When the friends were scourged by God they took the right attitude and did not get into despair. If the scourge of eternal reality comes, see that it leaves you face to face with God, not with yourself.

The Surgery of Events Reacting (Job 42:8)

Therefore take unto you now seven bullocks and seven rams, and go to my servant Job, and offer up for yourselves a burnt-offering; and my servant Job shall pray for you: for him will I accept. (v. 8a)

We only see along the line of our prejudices—our evangelical or un-evangelical prejudices, the prejudices of our belief or of our agnosticism; we cannot see otherwise until events operate on us. The surgery of events is a most painful thing. It has taken a devilish thing like this war to root up the prejudices of men who were misrepresenting God to themselves. A prejudice is a foreclosed judgment without having sufficiently weighed the evidence. Not one of us is free from prejudices, and the way we reveal them most is by being full of objection to the prejudices of other people. If we stick obstinately to any line of prejudice, there will come the surgery of events that will shift us out of it. Watch that you do not make an issue with God; it is a dangerous thing to do.

The surgery of events brought the friends out of their prejudices. All along they had said to Job, "You are wrong, we can prove it, you are a bad man, and it is a wonder to us that God does not strike you dead." But the surgery of events brings them to their knees in utter humiliation. "Go to My servant Job," God says, "and he shall pray for you." "Go through the issue, or you will never get to Me." Think of the humiliation of it!

> . . . lest I deal with you after your folly, in that ye have not spoken of me the thing which is right, like my servant Job. (v. 8b)

What is it to speak "the thing that is right" (Job 42:7) about God? I have never seen God; to call Him omnipotent and omnipresent and omniscient means nothing to me; I do not care one bit for an Almighty Incomprehensible First Cause. To speak the thing which is right about God, I must be in living personal relationship with Him. God is riddling the friends because while preaching the right thing, they have misrepresented Him and told a lie about the Author of Truth. If I preach the right thing but do not live it, I am telling an untruth about God. This is one of the cardinal truths of Christianity (see Romans 2:17–23). "But," a man says, "how am I going to live the truth?" The Sermon on the Mount says we must have a disposition which is never lustful or spiteful or evil; where are we going to begin? Unless Jesus Christ can put into us His own heredity, it is impossible. But that is just what He claims He can do. By regeneration Jesus Christ can put into any man the disposition that will make him the living example of what he preaches. The baptism of the Holy Ghost did not add anything to the apostles' doctrine, it made them specimens of what they taught (see Acts 1:8).

The Sacrament of Experimental Repentance (Job 42:9)

So Eliphaz the Temanite and Bildad the Shuhite and Zophar the Naamathite went, and did according as the LORD commanded them.

The friends accepted the humiliation, and did a repentant thing.

Strictly speaking, repentance is a gift of God. No man can repent when he chooses. A man can be remorseful when he chooses, but remorse is a lesser thing than repentance. Repentance means that I show my sorrow for the wrong thing by becoming the opposite. The old Puritans used to pray for "the gift of tears." A man has the power to harden himself against one of God's greatest gifts. If in order to dissolve a piece of ice, you take a hammer and smash it up, you simply break it into so many pieces of ice; but put the ice out in the sunshine and it quickly disappears. That is just the difference between man's handling of wrong and God's. Man's handling may cause it to crumble, but it is only so much crumbled-up wrong; when God handles it, it becomes repentance, and the man turns to God and his life becomes a sacrament of experimental repentance.

These men did not say, "No, we will not go to Job"; they did not attempt to justify themselves, they did exactly what God told them to, and in so doing they did a grand and noble thing, and took the only chance of getting to know God.

The Supplication of Emancipating Religion (Job 42:10)

And the LORD *turned the captivity of Job, when he prayed for his friends. (v. 10a)*

Have you come to "when" yet? If you are in the position of Job and have shipped some trouble on board that makes you taken up with yourself, remember that when Job prayed for his friends, God emancipated him. Pray for your friends, and God will turn your captivity also. The emancipation comes as you intercede for them; it is not a mere reaction, it is the way God works. It is not a question of getting time for Bible study, but of spontaneous intercession as we go about our daily calling, and we shall see emancipation come all along, not because we understand the problems, but because we recognize that God has chosen the way of intercession to perform His moral miracles in lives. Then get to work and pray, and God will get His chance with other lives; you do not even need to speak to them. God has based the Christian life on redemption, and as we pray on this basis God's honor is at stake to answer prayer.

The Society of Enlarged Friendship (Job 42:10–17)

. . . also the LORD *gave Job twice as much as he had before. (v. 10b)*

Job's actual life looked exactly the same after his suffering as before to anyone who does not know the inner history. That is the disguise of the actual. There is always this difference in the man who has been through real trouble—his society is enlarged in every direction, he is much bigger minded, more generous and liberal, more capable of entertaining strangers. One of the great-

est emancipators of personal life is sorrow. After the war there
will be the society of enlarged friendship in many a life; men will
never be as estranged from one another as they used to be. One
thing which has gone by the board entirely is the conceit that we
know men. Men do not live in types; there is always one fact
more in every life that no one knows but God. The last thing to
go is the religious category. A man will stick to his religious cate-
gories of men until he receives a shaking up from eternal reality,
as these men did. Eliphaz and the others maintained the conception that unless a man held to the particular shibboleth of their
religious creed, he was lost. The one thing that will cause the
conceit that we know men to disappear is the surgery of events,
the eternal reality of God shaking the nonsense out of us. This
has happened in many a life through the cataclysm of war, and
men find they have a different and a broader way of looking at
things. There is no room for veneer and pretence in camp life.

Then came there unto him all his brethren, and all his
sisters, and all they that had been of his acquaintance before,
and did eat bread with him in his house: and they bemoaned
him, and comforted him over all the evil that the LORD had
brought upon him. (v. 11a)

There was a larger, grander society in Job's actual life after
his suffering. In his epistle Peter refers to the people who have
plenty of time for you, they are those who have been through
suffering, but now seem full of joy (see 1 Peter 4:12–19). If a
man has not been through suffering he will snub you unless you
share his interests, he is no more concerned about you than the
desert sand; but those who have been through things are not now
taken up with their own sorrows, they are being made broken
bread and poured-out wine for others. You can always be sure of

the man who has been through suffering, but never of the man who has not.

> *. . . every man also gave him a piece of money, and every one an earring of gold. (v. 11b)*

Job accepted the gifts from his friends and brethren, which is an indication of a generous spirit. The majority of us prefer to give, but Job was big enough to accept all that his friends brought him.

> *So the LORD blessed the latter end of Job more than his beginning. (v. 12)*

Notes

[1] The Imperial School of Instruction was established at Zeitoun (zay TOON) in September 1916 by the British Command to train troops primarily in infantry weapons and tactics.

[2] B. C., the initials of Biddy Chambers; although Mrs. Chambers was editor, compiler, and often publisher, she never identified herself by name in any of the books.

[3] Dinsdale T. Young (1861–1938) was a noted Methodist minister who influenced Chambers, especially during Oswald's years at Dunoon Theological College in Dunoon, Scotland (1897–1906).

[4] At Zeitoun, six miles northeast of Cairo, was a YMCA camp, the Egypt General Mission compound, and, from 1916 to 1919, the Imperial School of Instruction, a training base for British, Australian, and New Zealand troops during World War I.

[5] Throughout this manuscript *the war* and *this war* refer to World War I (1914–1918).

[6] The *ban of finality* means the limitation or curse of having one's mind made up, to the point of being unwilling to consider new information.

[7] Francis Bacon, *Essays* (1625), "Of Adversity."

[8] *Priggishness* is an annoying smugness in moral behavior and attitude.

[9] *Prig*: a person who is annoyingly smug in his or her moral behavior and attitude.

[10] This most likely is Thomas Henry Huxley (1825–1895), English biologist and teacher.

[11] F. W. H. Myers (1843–1901) was a British poet and educator.

[12] From the *Westminster Shorter Catechism of the Presbyterian Church.*

[13] Thomas Edward Brown (1830–1897) was a British poet.

[14] *Chattermagging*: jabbering; spouting off; rambling on.

[15] Alexander Whyte (1836–1921) was a Scottish minister who influenced Chambers during Oswald's time at Edinburgh University (1895–1896).

[16] *moloch*: a tyrannical power requiring sacrifice in order to be appeased.

[17] The phrase *took up the cudgels for* means *came to the defense of.*

[18] Giuseppe Mazzini (1805–1872) was an Italian patriot.

[19] P. T. Forsyth (1848–1921) was a British Congregationalist minister and theologian. Chambers read many of Forsyth's books and valued his insights.

[20] Ugo Bassi was a central figure in H. E. Hamilton King's epic, *The Disciples,* published in 1907.

[21] Matthew Arnold (1822–1888) was an English scholar, poet, and critic.

Note to the Reader

The publisher invites you to share your response to the message of this book by writing Discovery House Publishers, Box 3566, Grand Rapids, MI 49501, USA. For information about other Discovery House books, music, or videos, contact us at the same address or call 1-800-653-8333. Find us on the Internet at http://www.dhp.org/ or send e-mail to books@dhp.org.